More
Than
Dead Wood

Build Your Own Log Furniture

Les Smith • Dan Swesey
Illustrator Les Smith

Photography by:

Les Smith, Dan Swesey and Joe Blackstock

BUILD YOUR OWN LOG FURNITURE: TEN GREAT PROJECTS YOU CAN BUILD FOR FUN AND PROFIT First Edition

ISBN: 0-9707046-0-7

10 9 8 7 6 5 4 3 2 First Printing: January 2001

Printed by Graphcom Printers LTD. 1009 2nd Ave South Lethbridge • Alberta, Canada T1J0C8
     Cover printed on Kromekoteplus CIS Cover, interior pages Boise Opaque Book 70#

Library of Congress Card Number: 2001116140

Published & Distributed By:
Logman Furniture Co.
logman@notherntel.net
www.logmen.net

Acknowledgements

Authors: Les Smith • Dan Swesey

Book Design & Production:
Karin Hoffman
A. J. Images Inc.

Cover Design: Karin Hoffman

Cover Illustration: Les Smith

Illustration: Les Smith

Photographers: Les Smith, Dan Swesey
and Joe Blackstock

Special Thanks from Dan to:

My family for their never ending support.
Les for his vision & friendship.
Joe, *The tradin' king. Thanks for introducing me to Barnum*
Raul Bustamante, United Wood Products.
Marty, "Dan it's your time".
Karin at **A.J. Images Inc.,** for all her magic.
Look Out Below Productions,
Matt, Tera and the staff.
Dave at Masterfx, "you are the internet".
Denny, for the loan to buy my first set of tools.
The students I have had the privilege of teaching.
Praise God, from whom <u>all</u> blessings flow.

Special Thanks from Les:

Looking back, I now see that it was the situations and people that have come into my life that helped to make this book and video possible. A special group of positive people who participated, supported and encouraged me.

God
My new wife Grace, love, support and help with the book.
Dan & Judy, through good times and bad and sharing
the vision to the end.
Jack Forney, for his patients.
Joe, he is the real "Barnum"
Ryan, for help making the Montana transition.
Koookies and wine. Got any rock & roll?
Marty, Good food & Friendship
A. J. Images Inc., Karin, for bringing the vision out in the book.
Look Out Below Productions, two wonderful people with
a vision of their own.
Dave at Masterfx, for our internet.
Henry at **Minwax,** understanding our industry and helping
us to educate people.
All the students in Colorado and Montana,
thanks for the great memories.

Our Little Tradin' Post

Contents

Introduction

When someone mentions log furniture to you, what comes to mind? Watching old reruns of Bonanza? Wearing a coonskin cap when you were a kid, pretending you were Davey Crockett? Kicking back in a ski lodge or an old mountain cabin on a snowy day?

Let's be honest, log furniture represents much more than just a rustic-looking dresser or a one-of-a-kind bed. It communicates a way of life that is quickly fading away: a life that is simple and free of stress. A life where people trust each other unless proven otherwise. A life where neighbors help neighbors.

As our society grows busier and more complicated, people are looking for ways to escape the hustle and bustle of everyday living. They want a remote cabin or even a place in their home where time seems to stand still.

More than a piece of dead wood,
            as told by Les Smith

My adventure in building log furniture actually began while living in a remote mountain cabin 11,000 feet above sea level near Fairplay, Colorado. All my life I had wanted to get away from civilization and finally my dream came true. By day I worked in the construction industry, but when I came home, I lived a very simple life – miles away from my nearest neighbor – in a very rustic cabin. It was so rustic, in fact, that I had no electricity or running water. I chopped wood to "keep the home fires burning" in my potbellied stove and, when we needed it, I would haul in water. Some people might have felt sorry for me, but I loved it!! It has been said that my family is a direct descendent of Davey Crockett (my mother's maiden name is Crockett), perhaps my craving for "the wild frontier" came honestly.

While gathering firewood on a snow-covered mountain one spring day in 1991, I noticed a peculiar-looking tree laying on a pile of other dead trees. Over time, a persistent wind had created an interesting series of bends in the wood. That looks like a bench! I thought to myself. It didn't really look like a bench, but for the very first time in my life I saw the tree as something more than a piece of dead wood. This is a tree with personality!

I dragged the tree back to my cabin, stripped the bark off and fashioned it into a bench which sat in my family room (if that's what you would call the little room in my cabin). A few years later when I sold my home, the buyers liked the bench so much they insisted I include it as part of the cabin.

Branching into something different

Working on that bench whetted my appetite for building log furniture. After experiencing some family crises, I knew I needed to make a change and branch into something different – so I decided to start making log furniture. Unfortunately, I couldn't find any books that explained the craft, so I resorted to the oldest method of building known to man: trial and error. And let me tell you, when I started I made more than my share of mistakes!

In the beginning I made rustic bunk beds and advertised them in the classified section of the Denver newspapers. To my surprise, people actually found my little ads and bought them! I converted a storage unit into a makeshift workshop and expanded my product line to include rustic bent log aspen beds which are still our most popular sellers.

If the furniture I built wasn't already spoken for, I set them up on the side of a busy road with a sign giving my phone number. Despite being exposed to the elements, the furniture never sat long enough to get worn and dirty.

Soon, people began asking, "Is there any way you could custom-make some furniture for me?" Having experimented with different approaches to design as well as tenon and mortise construction , I figured, Why not?

My workload increased and back orders began piling up so I taught other people what I had learned and hired them to help shoulder the load. Today, we sell log furniture through our Denver store, Cowboy-Up, and I spend the majority of my time doing what I love –building log furniture. My partner, Dan, joined me to build log furniture and make sure the operation runs smoothly.

Sharing the wealth

Some people who walked into the shop weren't interested in having us build log furniture for them – they wanted to enjoy building it themselves. We shared with them what we had learned and they gladly went on their way. Finally we decided to offer a beginners class in conjunction with a local university. Hundreds of students later, we decided to develop an instructional book and video series.

As word spread that we were developing the series, people asked us, "Why would you create competition for yourselves?" Dan and I don't see it that way. First of all, as I mentioned earlier, building log furniture represents a simpler time – a time when people shared what they learned with one another. Second, we believe getting as many people as possible interested in log furniture will only strengthen the industry and make our products even more popular!

What you will discover in this book

The purpose of this book is to show you how to Build Your Own Log Furniture using basic hand and power tools. Using the techniques described in the following pages, even a novice can build log furniture with little difficulty.

The quality of furniture you build will be reflected in the materials and tools you have on hand. If you are willing to learn how to use new and old tools alike, chances are you will become quite proficient in this craft.

Like us, trial and error will be your best guide, so be patient and keep a sense of humor. And we can't emphasize the humor enough. Every mistake and questionable-looking piece of furniture you build will make you a better craftsman; take it too seriously and you may get frustrated and quit. If it weren't for a sense of humor, our shop would have never survived.

Wood is very forgiving!

Knowing that no two pieces of log furniture will look exactly the same makes this craft very forgiving. If you cut a piece of wood wrong, don't be upset, just use it for something else. Around our shop, the builders joke that we need to declare up front what we are making before we begin because they often end up becoming something else. An entertainment center one of our carvers began building became an armoire dresser and then eventually a fish aquarium stand. Don't sweat it!

If you build a chair that sits sideways or leans too far forward, be encouraged that you are getting better. Just keep building until you get it right. Your first bed may take you three weeks but your next bed may only take you one week. Stick with it and eventually you'll be able to build a bed in a day. Stick with it too long and you might even write a better book than this one.

Whether you want to make this a hobby or earn a living at it, anyone can learn to build log furniture. Most people just need to see it done once and then they can duplicate the process. Don't be afraid to use your imagination. There really are no rules, so just have fun.

Researching this book was quite an eye-opening experience. One author believes you make a spiritual statement with every piece of furniture you build. Another author sees rustic furniture as a decorative form of rebellion against the excesses of civilization. We're not sure the first caveman or woman to go to the restroom while sitting across a bent bough would necessarily agree. We tend to believe that log furniture was born out of necessity, the availability of materials, and the creativity of each builder.

With the introduction of new tools and building techniques, this industry is constantly changing. We don't know everything nor do we presume to be the experts. There are hundreds of ways to build log furniture. We have found success and actually make a living at it, so we pass what we do know on to you.

Either way, here we are at the beginning of a new millennium building log furniture. At least we have that in common, so enjoy and good luck.

1 *Past and Present*

Log Furniture
of Yesterday

Log Furniture
of Today

Log Furniture of Yesterday

Heading west in covered wagons two centuries ago, the pioneers' didn't have room to bring their "traditional" furniture with them. When a family finally found the spot where they wanted to stake their claim and begin a new life, they had to literally start over. From the ground up.

Because they needed protection from animals and the elements, the pioneers' first order of business was to build a sturdy roof over their heads. Construction companies and lumber yards weren't available to the people whose closest neighbors may have been several miles away. So they created their new life around whatever resources were available. If they settled in the grassy flatlands between the Texas panhandle and the Dakota plains where trees were scarce, they built sod houses out of the prairie grass.

But if the settlers lived in or near a forest, then they used their ready supply of wood. After clearing the immediate area of rocks, brush and trees, they walked through the forest looking for fallen logs to build their cabin.

Building furniture

After constructing a home and developing a steady source of provision, the pioneer settlers could begin furnishing their homes. On the plains, the best source for the limited supply of trees was by the nearest river. Elsewhere, the settlers returned to the forest to find wood

for their furniture. They may have even used the left-over branches from the logs used to build their houses. The most common woods used at that time were pine, post oak, and aspen—just as they are today.

Saws at that time, like the one on the previous page, were extremely useful and saved time. Unfortunately, they were scarce and few settlers had them at their disposal. More important to the frontier family was the single-bladed ax below. Frontier families used this versatile tool to chop wood for houses and furniture as well as, firewood for cooking and heating. We'll look a little closer at the tools of yesterday in Section 2.

There's very little recorded history about log furniture because it was the common person's furniture. If you needed a chair, you built a chair. If you needed a table, you built a table. In the "olden" days, the cheapest way to get furniture was to make it yourself. If a lumber mill wasn't nearby, or you just didn't have the money to buy the lumber, you walked into the woods, found the right trees, and fashioned your own furniture to your liking, all the while using whatever tools they had on hand This is the very same technique we are teaching you.

Now let's look at a sample of the furniture from that time…

Log furniture was built for necessity

Look at this great old chair (see photos below)! Passed down through a family for at least three generations, it was built 70 to 100 years ago in South Dakota. With its most productive days behind it, the chair has been retired to an old grain bin in Montana that has been converted into a storage building.

This chair is still around because it was built to last, had a simple design, and was pleasing in the eyes of its owners. The craftsman who built it probably knew a little about logs, had some tools and needed a chair. Take a close look at the photo on the opposite page and you will see it was assembled with black lag bolts!

Taking a closer look at the rack (see photo below), notice how the craftsman creatively connected the two naturally formed "Y" shaped logs together. Next, he attached two logs at the base for stability. The cross pieces or rungs have a tenon on each end and were likely shaped with a draw knife. You can tell a draw knife was used because each piece is marked with flat edges. Notice that the tenons are tapered! A hole, or mortise, was drilled and the log ends were then tapered to fit tightly into the hole.

The newspaper/magazine rack shown below was also built 70 to 100 years ago in South Dakota by the same unknown craftsman who made the chair. There was a need for a rack to hold items such as: magazines, sheet music, and books etc..

The photo to the left depicts a very old, unique bent log lamp that now sits in the upstairs loft of an old Quonset. Notice the wonderful shapes and colors of the wood. The feet to a lamp like this (bottom left) will *never* be replicated. Most log furniture designs are unique and one of a kind. This is definitely one of them!

For our last picture (seen above: Toilet paper holder) we have an item that isn't real old, but it *is* very creative and most likely built out of necessity. Notice that a horse bit with a stick through the holes holds the roll of toilet paper. Look closely at the upper left hand corner of the picture, and you will see a bird perched on an adjacent branch. The bird didn't pose for the picture—it's permanent.

Now that we've looked at furniture in the past, let's look at furniture in the present.

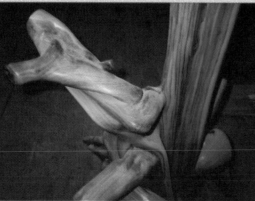

Special thanks to Robert Winkowwitsch for allowing us to photograph the old lamp for use in our book.

Top left: **Bar Stools** with back, Aspen
Above: **Bar Stools,** Pine

Top right: **Captain Chair**, Pine & Aspen Skip Peel.
Lower right **Storage Bench** with back, Pine & Aspen.

Previous page: **Aspen Collection**
Half Canopy Bed, Lowboy & Tall Dressers, and Amour

Left: **Writing Table and Chair**
Table has a pine top, half round pine drawer front with an aspen drawer pull. Legs and cross supports are aspen as well

Right: **Tall Boy Dresser**
featuring six Cedar drawers with aspen top, pulls, corner logs and trim.

Below: **Low Boy Dresser**
featuring eight Cedar drawers with aspen top, pulls, and corner logs.

Below: **Cedar Chest**
features Air-o-matic cedar with Felt lined tray, trimmed in aspen and pine.
it measures 24" x 36" by 24" high.

Left: **Nightstand**
featuring two drawers with
aspen top, pulls,and legs.
top is 21" x 21" by 28" high.

Right: **Shelf style Nightstand**
pine top and shelf, aspen legs.
top is 21" x 21" by 28" high.
Note the pine bark that ads
character and personal style

**Custom Built
Grandmother
Clocks**
By: Jerry Swesey
(Dan's Dad)

Left: **Aspen**
with clear finish

Right:: **Ponderosa Pine**
made from
Beetle Kill Blue Stain

Top: **Picnic Table with 4 benches,** Pine.

Top: **Dinning Table with six chairs,** pine table is 72" x 36" and 30" high.

Below: **Hutch and buffet** Custom made for the client in four sections. Pine and aspen construction, featuring five drawers, four glass doors, four solid cubbord doors and aspen pulls.

Top left: King **Canopy Bed,** aspen featuring an attached bench.

Below: **Queen Canopy Bed,** aspen

Nightstand with one drawer and shelf, pine & aspen. Custom **Reading Chair** with matching **Footstool,** pine.

Below: **Queen Bed,** pine

featuring smaller, straighter spindles and a beautiful "Gnarl" or "Burl" in the center of the headboard.

Above: **King and Queen Beds,** aspen

These are some very wild and creative aspen beds. Have fun, be as creative as your mind allows.

Above: **Bear bench,** pine

Right: **Rocking horse,** aspen

Above: **Rustic Entertainment Center,** pine.

2 Tools

Tools of Yesterday

Tools of Today

Our Toolbox

General Supplies

Tools on the hood of this truck are some of the tools of yesterday. They were used to create a roof over your head or a chair to sit on.

The brace has been used for years and is still being used today. If a craftsman needed to drill a hole, he would use a brace. Drop in his drill bit, tighten and begin boring a hole.

For best results, use an auger or an expansion bit. The threads on the tip of the bit will help pull the bit into the wood. To gain respect for the old craftsman, try using some of the old tools which can still be found in second hand stores, antique shops and at flea markets.

Auger bits were tools of yesterday and they are still popular
today because they cut a
clean hole fast.

The threaded point pulls the cutter
through the wood as the auger,
which is a part of the bit, feeds the
chips and sawdust up and out of the hole.
They may be sharpened and should last quite a
long time.

An Expansion bit is a cutter that was used
yesterday and today. This bit also has a
threaded point that is very
effective in pulling the cutter in a straight line through
the wood. The advantage is that
it can be adjusted to cut different
size holes up to 3 inches in diameter. On the
other side of this
cutter is a slot screw that can be
tightened and loosened to adjust the
cutter in and out.

A drawknife is a very effective tool for cleaning the bark off logs. It is also a tool that was used yesterday and we still use them in our shop today. The most effective way to use the knife is to put the beveled edge down against the log and hold onto each handle, then pull back toward your body. Certain types of drawknives can be used with the flat side down. The beveled edge needs to ride on the surface of the log. The amount of bark taken off depends on the cutting edge of the drawknife. Tilt the cutting edge when handles are lowered down. This takes off more bark. To take off less bark, raise the handles. This lets the blade lay flatter against the log. Practice makes perfect. The better peeling job that is done, the less sanding and grinding that will need to be done later.

The "Adz" was used to chip out or "saddle notch" the log. This technique was used to connect the logs and tie in the corners in log cabins. this tool is still used today. A hatchet was probably the tool of choice before some bright lad invented the Adz.

Tools of Today

"An important note from the authors"

Tools of today make it easier and faster to build log furniture. If you're just getting started don't assume you need to buy every tool listed in this chapter. Use your creativity and good old fashioned ingenuity to make use of the tools you already have.

Saw Tooth "Bur Bit" Forstner

Tenon Cutter

Dowel Plug Cutter

Japanese saws are very effective in doing several tasks because they are flexible and strong and make a nice, clean cut. In our shop we use them to cut off the excess part of a dowel, so it is flush with the log.

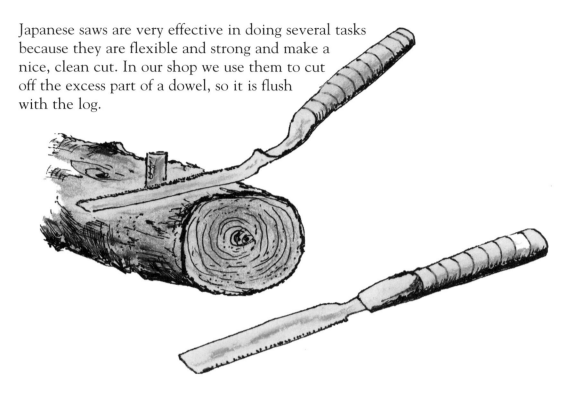

Wood chisels are used to chip away any rough spots, bark, high edges, etc.. We also use a chisel to chip away dry glue in tight places.

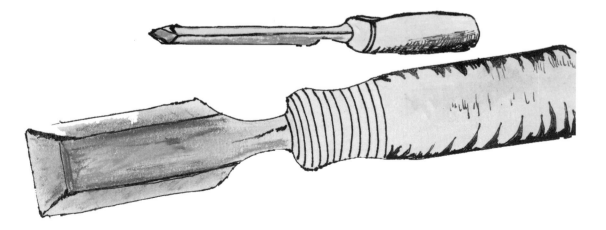

ORBITAL SANDER   DW420

This tool is a must for your shop. Hardly a day goes by that we don't work this tool. This is the quickest way to hand sand your pieces. It is well balanced which reduces fatigue and wrist cramp.

The model shown does not have a dust bag, this allows unrestricted access in tight areas. We use adhesive backed sanding disks, not Velcro backed disks.

4 $^1/_2$ ANGLE GRINDER   DW402

4-1/2" RUBBER BACKING PAD

DW4945

4-1/2" ABRASIVE DISK

LOCKING NUT

(supplied with DW4945)

W/ RUBBER BACKING PAD DW4945

One of the most versatile woodworking tools available, the angle grinder with rubber backing pad, is perfect for log crafting. From knocking down rough spots to feathering out and even stripping bark completely off the log. You can shape tenons with this tool,

grind down excess doweling, even make ugly spots disappear. The abrasive disks are available in several grits, ranging from 24 to 120 and higher.

To outfit your grinder with a rubber-backing pad, you will need an extended locking nut. DeWalt packages both backing pad and locking nut in one package, making it easy to convert your grinder. With other grinders you need wrenches to change grinding disks, but with DeWalt you just push a button and change out your disk.

HALF INCH DRIVE DRILL   DW239 & DW140

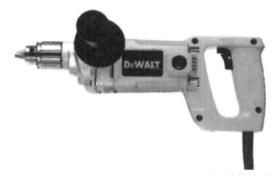

Since most cutting tools have a half-inch diameter shank you're going to need a half-inch drive drill. We have listed two models for consideration. The smaller drill is used for 3/8 inch and 5/8 inch auger bits. We also use this drill for smaller forstner/saw tooth bits. The smaller drill has a faster RPM than the larger drill and is easier to maneuver.

The larger drill has an end handle for better control when drilling with larger bits and cutting tools. This drill has a lower RPM than the smaller drill but has substantially more torque. The larger the bit, the slower the RPM should be. This factor will save you from twisting your wrist if the bit binds and suddenly stops. We recommend you consider using both styles.

HALF INCH IMPACT WRENCH DW290

Predominately used in bed making, the impact wrench is perfect for running the four lag bolts that are used in assembling log beds. Shorter lags are often used to connect tops as well as anchor table legs. This tool is capable of improving your speed and quality.

TRIM/SKILL SAW   DW936

This tool has proven to be a major time saver. With more power than you probably imagine, we can't say enough about this saw. We have used this saw to rip an eight foot, 2 inch thick rough sawn board with no problem. Perfect for making tops, you chalk a line and letter rip.

JIG SAW   DW321

The jig saw is primarily used for making the cut in the seat piece that fits around the post of the chair. There are other applications, but for the most part, this tool is a problem-solving tool.

HAND PLANER   DW680K

Great for leveling out and adjusting tops for a flush surface. Rough sawn timber tops have a tendency to warp. This hand planer will quickly make that problem disappear.

THICKNESS PLANER

Good rustic rough sawn lumber is not always the same thickness. That's **no problem** for this portable thickness planer. Set it to the desired thickness and run them through. It's a great tool for tops of all kinds.

MITER SAW DW708

This 12-inch saw is what makes every shop complete. From building log beds to custom dressers, this tool does it all. This saw will cut a 5-inch diameter log without any struggle. We highly recommend this saw.

TABLE SAW   DW744

The quality of all our case goods increased when we got this table saw. Totally user friendly and powerful, this tool of today is a great addition for any work shop.

ROUTER DW610

From inlays to carving cabin and road signs this tool has proven extremely valuable to have in our tool arsenal.

BAND SAW

Delta makes a great line of Band Saws that work excellent for building log furniture. From tapering logs to splitting logs, from cutting wood dowels to putting a flat siding on a drawer pull, a band saw does it all. If time is money, this tool is pure dollars. Remember that your tools will dictate your quality and speed.

CHAIN SAW

Probably the most necessary tool you will need. We recommend using a STILL Chain saw. The 020T is lightweight but has ample power and is easy to work with.

One of the newest tools for putting a tenon on a log is the **LOGMAN TENON MAKER** shown below. All you need is a router that has a 1/2" Collet. Attach your router to the tenon maker and start making tenons. The LOGMAN TENON MAKER puts tenons on hardwood logs and makes any length radius shouldered tenons. The carbide tipped router bit comes with the tenon maker. This new tool was invented by Les Smith and is used in his shop. The LOGMAN TENON MAKER is available at the companies listed below.

www.treelineusa.com   1-800-598-2743
www.loghomestore.com 1-800-827-1688
www.rockler.com   1-800-279-4441
www.baileys-online.com 1-800-322-4539

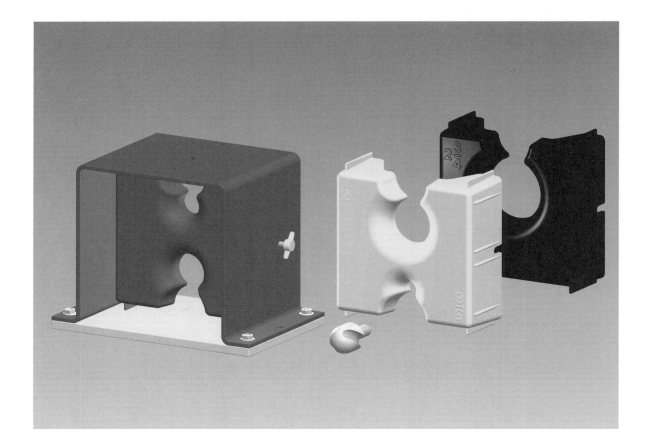

Our Tool Box

Hand Tools	Check list
Carpenters Hammer	☐ _____
Rubber Mallet	☐ _____
Sledge Hammer	☐ _____
1" Chisel	☐ _____
Chalk Line	☐ _____
Square	☐ _____
3 ft. Level	☐ _____
Ratchet straps (various sizes)	☐ _____
Hand Plainer	☐ _____
5 ft. Bar Clamps	☐ _____
C-Clamps (various sizes)	☐ _____
Table Top Vice	☐ _____
8" Drawknife	☐ _____
Hatchet	☐ _____
Barbed Riflers	☐ _____
Sharpening Stone	☐ _____

Cutting Bits

3\8" Auger Bit

5\8" Auger Bit

1 1\2" Tenon Cutter

1 1\2" Dowel Plug Cutter

2 5\8" Dowel Plug Cutter

2 5\8" Saw tooth forstner Bit

1 1\2" Saw Tooth forstner Bit

Power Tools

Orbital Sander

41\2" Angle Grinder w/Backing Pad

Half inch drive drill

Half Inch Impact Wrench

Trim Saw/ Skill Saw

Jig Saw

Band Saw

12" Chop/Miter Saw

Table Saw

Chain Saw

Router

Check list

☐ _____

☐ _____

☐ _____

☐ _____

☐ _____

☐ _____

☐ _____

☐ _____

☐ _____

☐ _____

☐ _____

☐ _____

☐ _____

☐ _____

☐ _____

☐ _____

☐ _____

☐ _____

General Supplies

Check list

Dowel 3\8"	☐ _____
Dowel 5/8"	☐ _____
Wood Screws 1"	☐ _____
Wood Screws 2"	☐ _____
Wood Screws 3"	☐ _____
Wood Glue	☐ _____
Black Markers	☐ _____
Pencils	☐ _____
Sanding Disks 80 grit	☐ _____
Grinding Disks	☐ _____
36grit	☐ _____
60grit	☐ _____
80grit	☐ _____
120grit	☐ _____
220grit	☐ _____
Sand Paper	☐ _____

Dust Mask ☐ _____

Ear Protection ☐ _____

Eye Protection ☐ _____

Leather Gloves ☐ _____

Paint Brushes ☐ _____

Bucket ☐ _____

Boiled Linseed Oil ☐ _____

Paint Thinner / Mineral Spirits ☐ _____

Sanding Sealer ☐ _____

2 Cycle gas mix ☐ _____

Gasoline ☐ _____

Bar Oil ☐ _____

Half inch x 5 1/2" lag bolts (Beds) ☐ _____

Half Inch Washers (Beds) ☐ _____

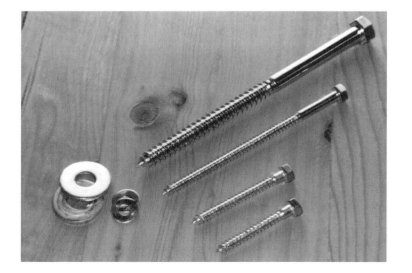

3 Getting Started

Logs & Materials

Sourcing logs can take some time and determination. If you already have a source for logs, you're ahead of the game. If you do not have a source, we hope this section will assist you in acquiring some.

We recommend using softwood. Lumber is typically categorized as hardwood or softwood. Broad leaf trees are considered hardwood while wood from cone-bearing trees is considered softwood.

Diamond Willow, *above*

Pine, *below*

Examples of softwood include Douglas-fir, ponderosa pine, yellow pine, western red cedar and other true fir trees. There are many geographical and territorial names given to pine and that can be confusing. If they call it pine, go with it as a soft wood source.

Those of us living in Colorado have the pleasure of working with aspen. Also known as Quakie or American Aspen this tree belongs in the populous family and is considered softwood. These trees offer a wood with quite a bit of character, bends, arches, twists and turns, not to mention bumps, beautiful gnarls, catpaws and colors. Some of nature's finest work

Aspen, *above*

comes in the form of aspen. If you have access to Aspen, your designs will have a special rustic quality.

Dry wood is the key. If you build with wet materials, not only will it be heavy, it will

American Aspen Leaf
"Quakie"

shrink and can have a high content of sap. If you are fortunate enough to harvest standing dead trees, this will eliminate most of these problems. When purchasing pine logs, or any logs for that matter, ask if they are wet or dry logs. The drying time depends on several factors. Know, the dryer and more arid the climate, the faster the logs will dry.

Wood is only as dry as the air that surrounds it, and once dried does not always mean it will stay that way. The moisture content of the wood changes with humidity. In southern states with high humidity you find wood with a high moisture content. When the rain or snow comes, we have to wait a few days to pull from our outdoor stock. Some of our rough sawn boards will expand almost a quarter inch after a hard rain.

Finding ways to dry your wood is important. There are three factors you need to control, humidity, air movement and temperature. If stacking your logs outdoors won't work in your climate conditions, you may need to look into building a dry kiln, or some other type of dehumidification process. The library is a great source to learn more about kiln drying wood.

Wood is dried to prevent checking and the yield to a lumber mill can be significantly reduced by

checking however, we are using the whole log and not just a cut out of the middle. Every log we build with has some sort of checking. If the checking is minor, we know the process is just beginning. If we see major checking, and bark starting to peel off, we know it's getting close, and that most of the moisture is out of the wood.

The drawing below is an illustration of "checking". You can see the growth rings and the  crack. The crack is called checking. This in most cases will not affect the structural integrity of the log. Position the checks away from tenon and mortise joints. Large checks should be positioned to the underside facing down or to the back of the piece that faces the wall, such as the back of the headboard Removing the bark from the logs will allow them to dry faster, see Drawknifing pg 29.

Knowing the moisture content of the wood is very important. A living tree's weight is over 50% moisture. Using wood with too much moisture can split, warp, cup, causing your joinery to loosen. Any one of these problems can ruin hours of hard work. Once you work with dry materials, you will better understand the difference.Having worked with commercial materials most of our lives, moisture has never really been much of a factor. Pulling timbers out of the forest is quite a bit different than pulling 2X4 studs off the pallet at your local lumberyard. In short, we recommend a **moisture meter.** This small investment is a small price in the pursuit of getting it done right the first time. Or you can use the following formula and calculate the moisture content for yourself.

It works like this:

Weigh the wet log

Dry the log till it no longer loses weight. This is the dry weight

Subtract the dry weight from the initial wet weight.

Divide the difference by the dry weight.

Multiply that sum X 100 = percentage of moisture.

This process is not real practical except for researchers and scientists. It is the most accurate method, but a moisture meter is accurate within a percent or two, and is quick and easy to use.

Rough sawn lumber, un-edged boards, single edge boards, barnwood and slabs are great material to work with. Table tops, bench tops and all kinds of dressers and case goods are built with this type of material. Typically, we deal directly with a lumber mill for this type of material. There are some great portable saw mills available that are more than capable of milling

rough sawn lumber. Sometimes you can find someone advertising milling services. Check the bulletin boards at lumber yards and mills.

Old barns can also be a great source for lumber. Especially, if you're capable of tearing it down and hauling it away. Fence companies can also be a great source for old weathered wood.

Sawmills are an excellent source for wood, slabs, logs and un-edged boards. Take the time to visit a Sawmill in your area, there is nothing like a first hand look. Ask as many questions as you can, most of the people we have met are willing to help. It may turn out that they will sell you materials or they can connect you with someone who can.

This particular mill is located in Whitlash, Montana. North Star lumber opened in 1982 and is owned and operated by Mark Engstrom.

Mark Engstrom and his son Zeb

Mark built this mill, which is not an easy task considering all the components and parts that make up this mill.

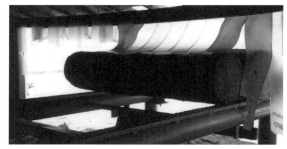

The hydrolics that move the logs and position the material are powered with a diesel engine.

A series of rollers helps move the timber through the mill. A forty horsepower electric motor runs the 20 foot long, 5 inch wide, 19 gage band saw blade. This saw mill will cut

3,000 board foot per day. Mark's mill can rip timbers 30 inches in diameter and in sections up to 21 feet long. Mark cuts Lodge Pole, Douglas Fir and Spruce. All three are in the pine family.

Placing a classified ad in the newspaper is another way to source wood. The example below is an ad placed in the firewood section of the classifieds. These ads will generate calls from all types of sources. Homeowners that cut down tress around their home would probably give you the logs just for hauling them away. A private landowner may have 50 acres of trees and would jump at the chance to thin out the dead trees in exchange for the logs. This would be a great opportunity.

Examples of Classified Ads

We buy dry, aspen and pine
logs, 8ft. lengths. you deliver
303.755.7990

Will thin cut, and haul away.
standing dead trees
303.755.7990

Call people selling firewood and ask if they can help you source wood. Arrange for them to deliver you a load of logs. Building as much furniture as we do, we can't afford to harvest our own wood, it is more economical for us to pay to have it cut and delivered.

Check with your local forestry division and obtains firewood permit. There may be some limitations with this agency, but is a great source of wood for you. On page 143 is a list of state foresters and forestry associations that can help or visit their website, a list is on page 139.

Wood Saw Horse

The Wood Saw Horse can be used for: cutting, peeling, drilling, sanding, etc.. Notice the ratchet strap. The strap can be tightened around two cross pieces on the horse and around the log. This is effective in keeping the log from moving.

To build this horse, follow the directions below.

- Cut four 2X4's 42" in length for two ends. Measure up 35" center where 2x4's cross. Nail or put in a deck screw. Measure 33" inside to inside at base. Then put in a nail or a 2nd deck screw at the cross.

- Cut two 2x4's 48" in length for two cross pieces. Nail or screw to top on each side to hold ends together.

- Rough cut your two angle pieces 54" in length. Nail or screw. Cut off excess butt ends that hang over ends.

This hog trough design is an excellent work station for peeling logs. It's just two pieces of wood nailed together. It has a sufficient backstop, a sturdy bottom board in which to rest the log.

This station should be just below hip height. Secure the peeling station to a table top or workbench in your shop area or outside under the shade of a tree. Use lag bolts and a sturdy post, this station should not move.

Tip:

Place your hip and body weight here.

This will free your hands to use the drawknife.

Vise

A vise is an important tool to have as one of your work stations. The vice must be securely mounted . We have found it's best to attach the vise to a large stump about hip height. When you work with any piece of wood, especially logs, ensure the log will not spin loose. Don't worry about the mark the vice will leave, you can sand it off later. Logs that move cause accidents and can damage your cutting tools. Check it twice, and you'll never be sorry.

Tenon & Mortise

The tenon, pronounced ("Ten - in"), and the mortise ("mor - dus"), is the type of joint used to join log furniture together. A tenon is basically a dowel and the mortise is a hole. The diameter of the tenon and the diameter of the hole should measure the same. The length of the tenon and the depth of the mortise should also measure the same. If you want an extra snug fit, you can drill the mortise $1/16$" smaller than the diameter of the tenon.

Ensure the mortise drill bit matches the diameter of the tenon. $1/8$" larger or smaller and and the tenon won't fit the mortise properly.

The three types of tenons we use are shown below.

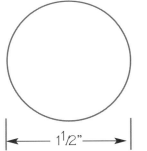

Mortise Depth & Diameter is $1\frac{1}{2}$"

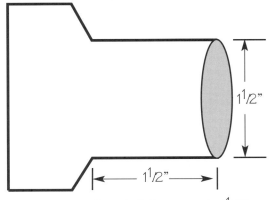

Mortise Depth & Diameter is $1\frac{1}{2}$"

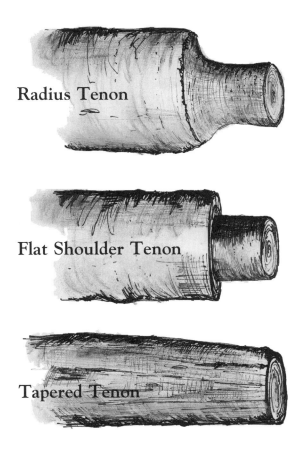

Radius Tenon

Flat Shoulder Tenon

Tapered Tenon

How you make the tenons depends on what tools you have. Below are eight tools which can be use to make tenons and the kind of tenons each tool can make.

- Drawknife
  Produces a tapered tenon.

- Hatchet
  Produces a tapered tenon.

- Lathe
  Produces both flat shoulder and radius tenons.

- Band Saw W/ Angle Grinder
  Produces a radius tenon.

- Hole Saw
  Produces a flat shoulder tenon.

- Hand Planer
  Produces a tapered tenon.

- Dowel / Plug / Cutter
  Produces a flat shoulder tenon.

- Tenon Cutter
  Produces a radius tenon.

The fastest and most consistent way to make a tenon is with a tenon cutter. A tenon cutter allows you to regulate the length of the tenon, and it will always give you a consistent tenon diameter. Tenon cutters are available in different diameters. The most common sizes are 1", $1^1/2$", and 2".

In addition to the tenon and mortise, dowel the tenon to the mortise to prevent it from pivoting or pulling apart. See Doweling pg 57

If you use your creativity building log furniture, you will use very bent and twisted logs. Length and diameter of your tenons are important, but the angle or lack of angle is critical. Drill the tenons "in line", see illustration below.

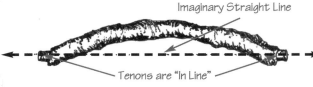

Imaginary Straight Line

Tenons are "In Line"

- NOTE: The tenons follow the imaginary straight line. They do not follow the arch or curve of the log.

The length of your tenons should be $1^1/2$ to 2" long. Any shorter and you might not get a real strong joint. Any longer and you risk the tenon having an angle you can't overcome. Every tenon you cut will have a slight angle. If you go to fit a spindle in and it does not line up with your holes, twist or turn the spindle and at some point, it will line up. Twisting or turning will apply to every time there is tenon work in a project.

Length of the tenon also effects the doweling process. If the tenon is too short the dowel might not have enough tenon to grab on it's way through. The stronger the joints of the furniture, the better the chance it will last for generations. If your furniture pivots, creaks, or wobbles, it will eventually breakdown and become firewood.

We see other builders using wood screws, staples or nail brads to tie in or fasten their tenons. This may be quicker, but it will weaken over time and come loose. If the tenons are the right length, consistent in diameter, glued and doweled, you will build durable furniture in which you can be proud.

Several types of bits can be used to drill the mortise or hole. We suggest using a saw toothed Forstner bit. Forstner is pronounced (fours ñ ner). Normally these bits require a half-inch drive drill. What makes the drill a half inch drive, is that the chuck of the drill will open wide enough to hold a drill bit with a half inch round shank.

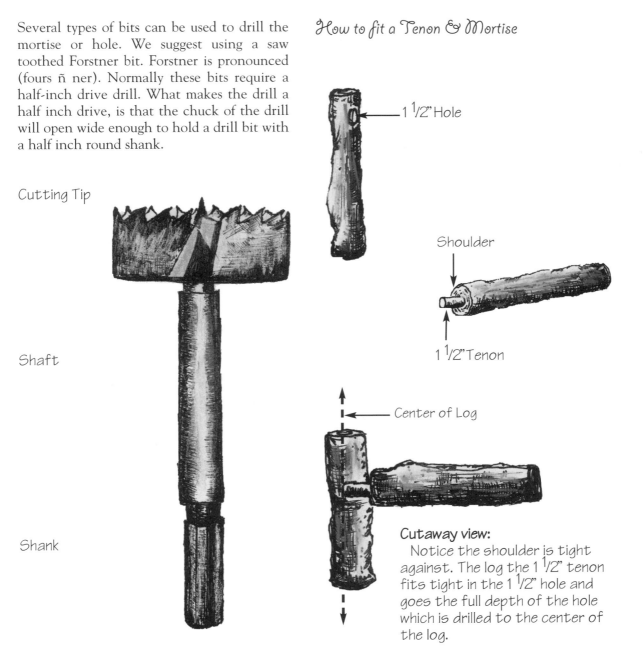

Cutting Tip

Shaft

Shank

1 $1/2$" Hole

Shoulder

1 $1/2$" Tenon

Center of Log

Cutaway view:
Notice the shoulder is tight against. The log the 1 $1/2$" tenon fits tight in the 1 $1/2$" hole and goes the full depth of the hole which is drilled to the center of the log.

These bits can be used in both a drill press and hand held drills. We also recommend you use a bit with a hexed shank as compared to a round shank. The round shank tends to slip in the chuck.

Doweling

oweling is tying or locking the tenon and mortise together. Done correctly, this type of joinery will last for generations. Doweling prohibits the joints from pivoting or pulling apart, and add's to the overall strength and durability of your furniture. Doweling is one of our best selling points and increases customer confidence. It is also the mark of a good crafter and should increase your confidence.

We use hardwood dowels 4-6 inches in length, in both 3/8 and 5/8 diameters. For smaller projects and diameter wood, we use the 3/8". For beds and larger diameter wood we use the 5/8". Doweling is available in other sizes as well. Keep in mind to use the same size auger bit with the same size doweling.

The trickiest part is drilling the hole for the dowel. Because you can't start the bit at an angle, you need to point the drill straight up and down. This is covered in our video. Once you begin drilling and the auger bit catches, the angle of the drill must be changed to

allow the drill bit to pass through the tenon and into the post. (See illustrations below)

Put glue on the dowel as well as a small amount in the hole you drilled. Pound the dowel into place and listen for a dull thud. That sound tells you the dowel is all the way in the hole. Don't keep hitting the dowel or it will be driven out the other side of your post.

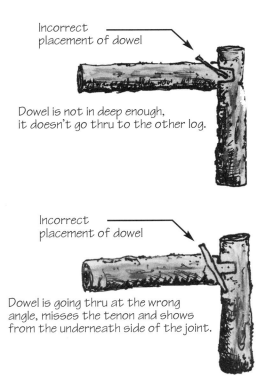

Incorrect placement of dowel

Dowel is not in deep enough, it doesn't go thru to the other log.

Incorrect placement of dowel

Dowel is going thru at the wrong angle, misses the tenon and shows from the underneath side of the joint.

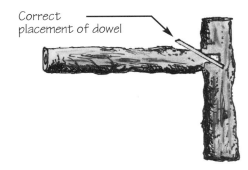

Correct placement of dowel

To cut off the excess dowel, use a grinder or saw and sand smooth to the touch.

A Speed trick for building furniture. Below is an illustration of two logs. Let's say that the logs are fixed in place and they "don't move". The trick is that you have to put a spindle or a rung in the holes where the tape measure is. If you were to measure all the way up inside the upper hole and all the way down to the bottom hole and then try to put the spindle or rung in, it could not be done. Do the following. Measure all the way into the top hole and measure down to the top face of the bottom log. As you can see in the illustration, this distance measures 8". Cut your log/spindle 8"long. Put a regular length tenon on the top end of the spindle and a short 1/2" to 3/4" tenon on the bottom end. Remember the bottom hole needs to only be about 1/2" to 3/4" deep. This will keep the spindle or rung from falling out completely once it has been dropped into the bottom hole.

Top log —

This hole has standard depth of 1 1/2" to 2"

the bottom hole needs to be only about 1/2" to 3/4" deep

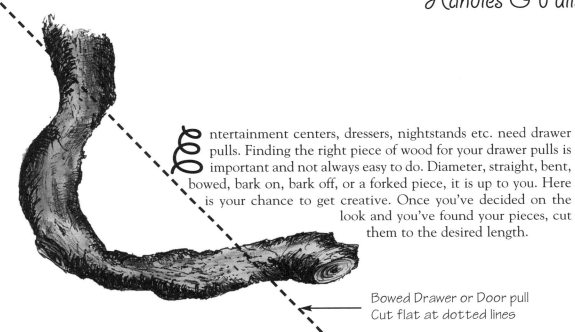

Entertainment centers, dressers, nightstands etc. need drawer pulls. Finding the right piece of wood for your drawer pulls is important and not always easy to do. Diameter, straight, bent, bowed, bark on, bark off, or a forked piece, it is up to you. Here is your chance to get creative. Once you've decided on the look and you've found your pieces, cut them to the desired length.

Bowed Drawer or Door pull
Cut flat at dotted lines

Cut or grind a flat surface on one side of the drawer pull. Using a band saw, a vise and chain saw or a vise and angle grinder can make this flat cut; this flat side will go up against the drawer or door surface. Sand and grind any sharp edge and round off both ends of each pull.

To attach:
1. Center the pull on drawer or door face.
2. Glue flat surface to the drawer or door front.

3. From inside the drawer or door, run two deck screws. If you are building with soft woods, and are using the proper length deck screw, don't drill a pilot hole.

aking a top to a bench, nightstand or table can be done in many different ways. For example, 2 X 6 boards can be joined by tongue and groove, biscuit joinery or doweling. There are several schools of thought on this issue and the library is a great source for carpentry information. However, there is little substitute for trial and error.

One point of agreement is all works best when you use dry wood. Make a top or two with wet wood and you will experience problems such as warping, splitting, cracking, and shrinkage just to name a few.

The following illustrations show how we build tops. A rule of thumb, is not to use boards any wider than six inches. Sometimes for benches we disregard this rule, but for the most part you will encounter fewer problems if you follow this rule.

The thickness of the material you are using, dictates the size of doweling you will use.

For the most part we use 3/8-inch doweling for building tops. Place dowels 6-8 inches apart on the length of the joining sides of the boards. Always measure down from the top surface to place the center of the dowel. (see illustration below)

The top surface should be as level and flush as possible. When building with rough sawn lumber, the boards are not always the same thickness. Measuring from the top down will increase your chances for a flush surface.

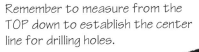

Remember to measure from the TOP down to establish the center line for drilling holes.

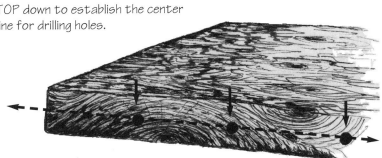

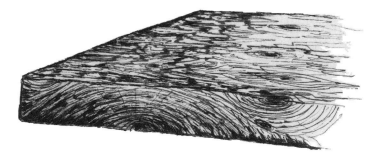

Drill your holes, with an auger bit as straight as possible, making sure the holes are deep enough for the dowels. If the holes are not deep enough the two pieces of wood will not come together. Glue all connecting surfaces and dowels.

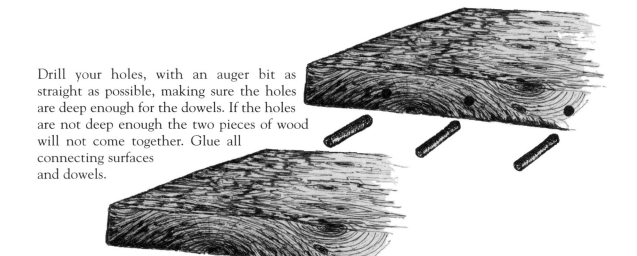

Use bar clamps to squeeze the boards together. The clamps should be tight, but don't over tighten or warping of the top may occur. Find the happy medium and allow the glue to dry.

To level any uneven spots, use a hand planer or an electric planer, belt sander or your angle grinder. Use whatever works best for you with the tools you have on hand.

Attaching Legs

There are four ways to attach legs to tops, tables, benches, etc.. The first illustration shows the hole drilled on the underside of the top where the leg tenon is the same size as the hole. The tenon goes in the full depth of the hole and the shoulder rests against the underside of the top. The tenon is glued and tapped into the hole. A counter sink hole for a lag bolt is drilled into the top. Make the counter sink hole deep enough for the head of the bolt and a wood plug. A flat washer should be used with the lag bolt to achieve greater strength.

top (side view)

Leg

The second illustration shows the tenon penetrating through the top.

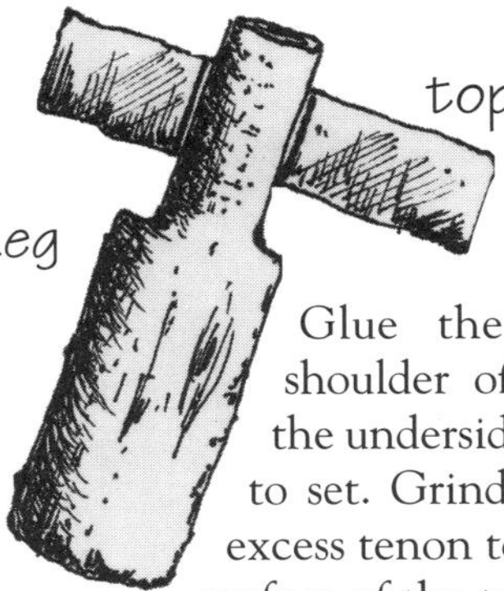

top (side view)

Leg

Glue the leg where the shoulder of the leg rests on the underside of the top, tap in to set. Grind and sand off any excess tenon to be flush with the surface of the top.

The third illustration shows how the leg fits tight into the hole made in the top. The shoulder of the leg again rests on the underside of the top. Apply glue in the hole and on the leg where the shoulder of the leg rests on the underside of the top.

top (side view)

Leg

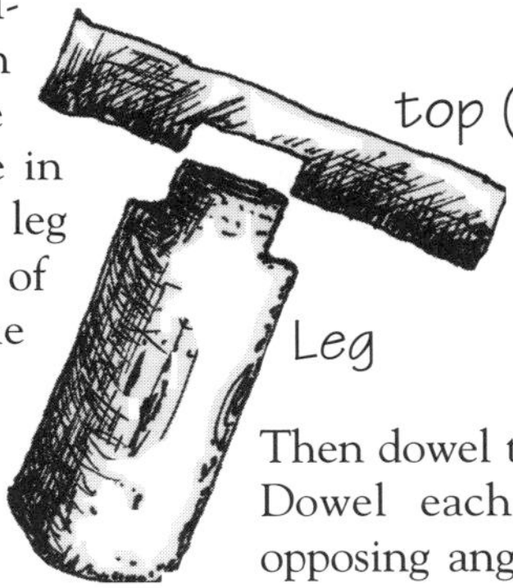

Then dowel the leg from the top. Dowel each leg at a slightly opposing angle to the other, this will secure the top to the legs.

The fourth illustration shows the leg is cut flat. No tenon - no hole. With an auger bit, drill a counter sink hole into the top deep enough for the head of a lag bolt, flat washer and a wood plug. Apply glue to the top surface of the leg. Place in position and attach to top with a lag bolt and flat washer, tighten up and tap in a wood plug.

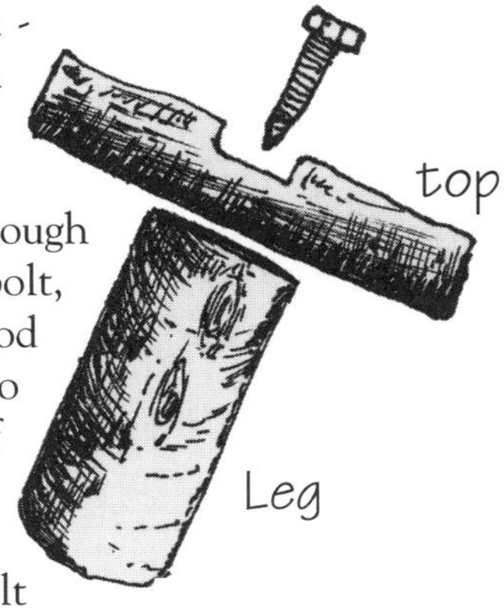

top (side view)

Leg

Finishes
Wood Stains
& Clear Protective Finish

After you have built your log furniture, you have a number of different options in enhancing and protecting its beauty. Log furniture has a unique charm of its own, which often lends itself to just a clear finish that will maintain the natural, rustic beauty of the wood. However, you may chose to add color and enhance the beauty of some pieces with a wood stain.

In this chapter we'll cover two methods for finishing your log furniture. First we've contacted the experts at Minwax who recommend the easy way to get great results using wood stains and clear finishes. Additionally, we'll cover some alternative methods we have used to finish log furniture including techniques utilizing boiled linseed oil, sanding sealers and waxes.

The Minwax Company has been in the business of making and keeping wood beautiful for nearly 100 years. They offer a full line of stains and clear protective finishes to satisfy all your wood finishing needs. Minwax also has an informative web site packed with wood finishing tips, product descriptions and numerous project ideas at **http://www.minwax.com**.

Preparation

Before starting any staining and finishing project, it is important to have a proper workspace. Choose a place that is well ventilated, dry, and warm, with good light. If there is ade-

quate ventilation, you can work virtually anywhere. If you put down heavy gauge plastic drop cloths, even a corner of the living room can become a temporary workshop. Your basement, attic or garage may meet your needs. However, if the area is cold or damp, the wood finishing products may require a longer drying time than the labels indicate.

Rubber gloves are recommended for keeping hands clean and protected. Old clothes are recommended because they are usually expendable and generally lint-free. This will help prevent fabric particles from getting stuck in the finish.

Finally, before starting almost any wood finishing project, the following items should be on hand: heavy plastic drop cloths and newspapers, rags, paint brushes (bristle and foam), #120 and #220 sandpaper, paper towels, Q-tips, mineral spirits, masking tape, and sealed metal containers, such as empty paint cans or coffee cans with lids (for cleaning brushes and, with the addition of water, for disposing of rags and waste soaked with oil finishes).

Sanding

Two crucial steps to a smooth attractive finish are:
1. Clean the bark off the logs thoroughly using a draw knife. Try to create as much of a "smooth to the touch" feel as possible.
2. Sand any high edges left by drawknifing. Round off and smooth sharp corners and rough spots. Lightly sand the wood in the

direction of the grain using a medium-grade sandpaper (#80 - #120) and repeat, working your way to a fine-grade sandpaper (#220).

When sanding is completed, wipe the surface of the furniture with a clean, dry cloth. Make sure the surface is dry, clean, and free of dirt, grease, glue and old coatings before finishing.

Many log furniture pieces are soft woods such as pine, alder, and aspen. To help ensure even stain color penetration and beautiful results, it is essential to pretreat soft or porous woods with *Minwax®, Pre-Stain Wood Conditioner*. This will help minimize any blotchiness that may occur.

Apply Minwax®, Pre-Stain Wood Conditioner, allow to penetrate 5-15 minutes, then wipe off excess with a clean, dry cloth. Apply stain within 2 hours of pretreatment.

✿ Tip:

To determine if you are working with soft wood, press your fingernail against a hidden section of the wood. If you make a dent, the wood is soft and needs conditioning.

Selecting & Applying a Wood Stain

Remember no two logs are exactly alike. Stains react differently to different types of wood. Before staining your project, test the selected stain on a hidden area of the wood or on a scrap piece of wood that is the same species as the furniture. This will ensure that you achieve the finished color you desire.

You can enhance the natural, rustic beauty of log furniture by imparting beautiful wood tone color. *Minwax® Wood Finish™, Minwax®, Gel*

Stain, and Minwax®, Pastels™ are penetrating stains that color and seal wood surfaces. *Wood Finish™* is available in 18 wood tone colors, and can be used to enhance any interior wood surface. *Wood Finish™* Natural is a great choice if

you opt not to change the color of the wood, but want to bring out the *natural* beauty of the grain. *Wood Finish™* is also available in a convenient aerosol spray. Offered in 9 of the most popular *Wood Finish™* colors, the new aerosol is perfect for intricately carved and hard-to-reach areas, and makes staining log furniture easier than ever. *Gel Stain* provides rich uniform color for wood, fiberglass, metal and other non-wood surfaces. The stain's gel form makes it ideal when working with soft woods like pine because it won't penetrate  too deeply into the wood's pores and cause blotching. *Gel Stain* has a convenient non-drip formula, which is great for vertical surfaces like doors and is available in 8 wood tone finishes. *Minwax®, Pastels®*, available in Winter White, is a penetrating stain that's ideal for  achieving an attractive *white wash* effect.

✿ Tip:

To help minimize wood swelling and shrinkage due to changes in humidity or temperature, apply stain and clear finish to all surfaces, even inside drawers, and under tables and chairs.

Selecting & Applying a Clear Protective Finish

While wood stains bring out the beauty of wood, clear protective finishes are essential for preserving and enhancing that beauty. Whether you choose to stain your log furniture or not, it is imperative that you protect the wood with a clear finish. A clear finish will protect your log furniture against water, household chemicals, food stains and wear. Just like the staining process there are a wide variety of clear finishes suited to fill your needs. To give furniture a durable finish, apply *Minwax® Fast Drying Polyurethane*, *Minwax® Polycrylic® Protective Finish*, or *Minwax® Wipe-On-Poly*.

Minwax® Fast Drying Polyurethane is the toughest topcoat for long-lasting protection. *Polycrylic®* is a hard, crystal clear, ultra-fast drying finish. Since *Polycrylic®* is water-based it is low odor, making it ideal for year-round use and easily cleans up with water. Both *Minwax® Fast Drying Polyurethane* and *Minwax® Polycrylic®* are available in a convenient aerosol spray. Log furniture is filled with twists, turns, nooks and crannies. Aerosol sprays are great for these hard to reach areas, and make getting a beautiful, smooth, protective finish easier than ever.

Wipe-On Poly, when applied with a soft, lint-free cloth provides hand-rubbed beauty and durable protection. Both *Fast Drying Polyurethane*

and *Polycrylic®* are available in Satin, Semi-Gloss and Gloss sheens. *Wipe-On Poly* is available in Satin and Gloss.

Tip:

-OR-

One-Step Finishes:

Some wood finishers like the convenience and the time savings that a *one-step* stain and finish product offers. *Minwax® Polyshades®* is ideal for the convenience-oriented finisher who is looking for rich stain color and polyurethane protection in one step. *Polyshades®* provides the beauty of rich stain and protection of polyurethane in one brush stroke. *Polyshades®* is available in 9 wood-tone colors in both gloss and satin finish.

Minwax® Woodsheen® is an easy-to-use rubbing oil. You can simply wipe on a stain and protective finish in one step achieving a beautiful, hand rubbed look. Available in seven colors, *Woodsheen®*'s ease of use and soft warm finish make a natural choice for log furniture.

Alternative Finishes

One of the finishes we use frequently use on log furniture is a boiled linseed oil and mineral spirits mixed 50/50. This is the first step on most of our furniture. For years, many people did not go beyond this first step because they liked the look. This mix will have a dull finish, but will bring enhance the darks and lights in the wood. Because this is an oil base mix (linseed oil), it tints the wood. The mineral spirits in this mixture thins the oil and helps it penetrate the wood. Eventually, the mineral spirits will evaporate. The more oil you use, the darker the wood will become.

Boiled Linseed Oil

Mix one part mineral spirits to one part boiled linseed oil. Boiled linseed oil has accelerators to speed up drying time. Raw linseed oil contains no accelerators and therefore, requires a longer drying time. Boiled linseed oil dries in 1 - 2 days, and raw linseed oil takes 4 days to a week to dry. Climate, humidity and the moisture content of your logs will effect drying time.

🌱 Note: manufactures recommend using raw linseed oil on children's furniture.

This linseed oil/mineral spirit mix can be applied several ways. It can be brushed, sprayed or rubbed on with a cloth or clean

shop rag. Be very careful if you apply with a cloth. Left in the direct sun, a cloth soaked in linseed oil can spontaneously combust and start a fire. You will also want to work in a well-ventilated area and wear a mask.

Referred to as an oil finish, this mix will bring out all the colors in the wood. Nothing brings out the colors in wood like an oil base finish. Furniture paste and wax finishes are oil based, which accounts for the rich look and spectrum of colors.

This oil finish left by itself with no topcoat or finish coat will dry to a dull finish. Dust will accumulate and is difficult to clean. This type of finish will need to be re-applied.

Sanding Sealers

If you are looking to put a durable smooth finish on your projects, sanding sealer is what is needed. We recommend sanding sealers be oil-based polyurethane. The advantage of using an oil base sealer is it brings out the color in the wood and retains that color when dry. Oil base sealers give a rich slight tint to the different cambiums in the wood grains. Oil base is combustible, so you need adequate ventilation. Avoid inhalation.

Water Based Sanding Sealers

Water based sanding sealers are also effective in putting a durable finish on wood. Today there are several new water based products on the market. The advantages are: fast drying, quick application, non-combustible, no dangerous fumes and easy cleanup. Some disadvantages are that in most cases, it must be sprayed rather than brushed and it requires direct application without an oil base first coat. Also, the finish tends to tint or cloud the rich tones and natural colors of the wood. Water base dies, artificial tints and stains can be added to the water base sealer to enhance and keep the color.

If you decide to use a linseed oil/mineral spirit mix for a first step, allow plenty of time for the oil base mix to dry. Have you ever tried mixing oil and water? It still doesn't work. Be patient and let the project completely dry. Then spray on a couple of quick coats of the water base sealer and you are ready for the final top coat. Test your chosen finish on a piece of scrap to ensure it is the color you want.

Sanding sealers do exactly what the name implies; they seal the wood. It fills and seals holes and lifts the pores of the wood. Once the sanding sealer dries you can run your hand across the surface and it will feel sandy, gritty and brittle. Using 220 grit sandpaper, sand the rough areas until they are smooth to the touch. Apply another coat of sanding sealer and let it dry.

Run your hand across the piece again and it should feel smooth. If not, repeat the process until you are satisfied.

Now that your project is smooth to the touch, you're ready to move onto a top or final coat. Shop around and ask questions. Some manufacturers have come up with a sanding sealer that works very well for either a topcoat or a final finish.

Wax Finishes

Another finish used today is wax. Wax puts a water resistant, dull finish on the wood and enhances the contrast between the light and dark areas of the grain. Applied with a cloth, this finish is very popular.

A wax finish on log furniture has a very appealing look. It's a natural finish that brings out the colors in the wood. Different waxes include beeswax, carnauba wax and paraffin wax. Some of the waxes should be considered a renewable finish. In time, some of the waxes will dull and another coat might become necessary.

Sometimes a coat of polish might help. Polishes and waxes have somewhat different functions as far as what they are meant to accomplish. Both are made to enhance a wood finish. You can find wax finishes in most major building supply stores. Wax comes in pastes, liquids and sprays. Read manufacturers directions for correct product application.

Some of the old furniture builders used their own mixture using beeswax and turpentine. After mixing, it was put in a metal can and warmed in hot water. Once hot enough, this mix turned into a paste which was then applied and left to dry for 5-15 minutes depending on the room temperature. When dry, it was buffed with a soft cloth.

Spraying

Spraying is the most efficient way to apply a finish to your furniture. You will not use quite as much product and is significantly faster. Spraying your finish will give you professional results. Prior to spraying, make sure all sanding is complete and your project is dust free.

Always read the manufactures label for recommended application instructions and warnings. You may find that certain finishes cannot be applied by spraying.

We recommend an easy spray turbine manufactured by Campbell Hausfeld. Their HV2000 series is cost effective and built to last. Campbell Hausfeld HVLP spray guns are designed to generate a high volume of low-pressure air. Turbines operate differently than conventional air compressors in that they do not require an air compressor to operate. This spray gun is portable and can be plugged into a standard outlet and sounds like a shop vac. The sprayer is lightweight and comes with a 15-ft. hose.

For more information about this sprayer, visit our web site at Hyperlink **http://www.Bestlogfurniture.net**

RUSTIC WESTERN ART

Rustic Western Art

Painting on wood using oil pastels and water based acrylic paints

Almost any wood is suitable for hand painting art work onto it in order to achieve an even more personalized rustic decorative piece. The sky's the limit, use your imagination when composing your creation on a rustic piece of furniture or wood. The first step is to envision the desired image as you would like it to appear on your project. Composition is often more important than craftsmanship so carefully consider content, placement and size of the image for your particular piece of wood. If your project or piece of wood is sanded and ready for a finish, then you are ready to start drawing.

Depending on your drawing skills, you may want to lightly sketch you vision directly onto your project or onto tracing paper using a #2 or #3 pencil. Remember, in either case you may want to make changes to your composition so the lighter you sketch the better. If you choose to sketch on tracing paper your completed drawing may be transferred to the wood by placing a piece of graphite paper between your drawing and the wood (graphite side down toward the wood) and then tracing over your drawing. As you trace, the graphite paper will transfer your marks to the wood. Graphite paper may be hand made or purchased from your local art supply store. If you choose to make your own graphite transferring paper it will take some time but once completed it will last for years. See the 🖌 Tip at the end of this chapter for instructions on how to make your own Graphite transfer paper.

Now that you have your composition on the wood, it's time to add some color. Oil pastels can be purchased from almost any craft or art supply store. Our graphic designer, Karin Hoffman of A. J. Images, who is also a fine artist, buys her materials on line from Dick Blick Art Materials. **www. dickblick.com.** She says they have just about everything an artist could want or need including some fine instructional books to perfect your talents.

If this is your first experience using oil pastels, you may want to experiment and become more familiar with the medium by practicing on a sanded scrap piece of wood. When practicing with the oil pastels discover how you can draw fine lines with the sharp edges and fill in large areas with the flat side. Practice blending and shading with your fingers applying different pressures against the wood. Rubbing or burnishing the oil pastel into the wood will help the wood retain the pigment. When you feel comfortable with this medium, apply what you have learned to your drawing on the project.

Below are two beautiful mountain scene illustrated on the top of a log benches.

When your pastel composition is the way you want it, you are then ready to start the protective finish process.

Apply boiled linseed oil and mineral spirits mixture (see finishes, boiled linseed oil page 70) over the entire wood surface, including your pastel composition, using a brush. The boiled linseed oil and mineral spirits will bring out the lights and darks in the wood grain and give the pastel drawing a slight amber tint. Allow one to two days for this finishing process to dry.

When the boiled linseed oil and mineral spirits mixture has completely dried, apply one coat of sanding sealer. (see finishes, sanding sealer page 71) When the sanding sealer is dry, lightly sand using 220 grit sanding paper.

Oil pastel drawing takes you through the first level in the process of painting on wood. In order to take your art to the next level, add more color to your composition and complete the process we have developed you will be using acrylic paints. Again, these can be purchased at the afore mentioned sources. Acrylic paints are fairly easy to work with even for the beginner. They are water-based and have a fast drying time. Familiarize yourself with this medium in the same manner you did with the pastels. Experiment with the paints on wood, canvas board, etc. Try mixing the paints to different degrees using different sizes and shapes of brushes or a pallet knife. Learn to create new colors. If you have the three primary colors (red, yellow and blue), as well as black and white you can mix any color your minds eye can imagine. For example, take a bit of yellow and add a bit of red to it and you will create, depending on the quantity of each, a variety of oranges ranging from red-orange to yellow-orange. If you add that color to white, you will lighten the value of the color producing a pastel shade, possibly for use in a sunset. On the other spectrum, adding black to the same orange color will deepen the value of the color for possible use on a tree trunk or rock. Books on this medium can be easily found at art-supply stores and public libraries.

After you have developed the acrylic painting techniques that satisfy you, it is time to paint onto areas of your rustic western art. Use the acrylic paints to add more color to your composition and paint in fine detail lines, as well as highlight areas that need to be brightened. There is no need to be concerned about the water based acrylic paints mixing with the oil pastels because we have coated over them with one coat of sanding sealer.

On this page are a few more samples of rustic western art on wood.

We wish you well. Take your time, have fun and enjoy the process of drawing and painting.

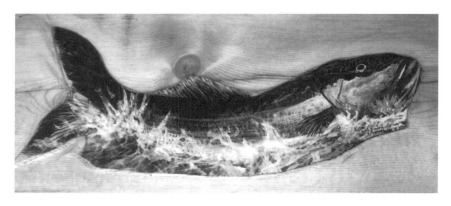

Tip:

Making graphite paper

Begin with a good size piece of tracing paper. Heavily coat one side with graphite using the softest (darkest) pencil you have available. Once you have coated your tracing paper with graphite use a cotton ball soaked in lighter fluid. Dab (don't rub) the soaked cotton ball onto the graphite until the paper is wet. Allow to dry completely. Repeat this graphite/lighter fluid /drying process to the same side of the paper several (5-6) times.

Use a 3/8 inch router bit to make cabin signs, Welcome signs, or personalize a bench like the one pictured above.

4 Marketing & Tradin'

"Gettin' your product to market...Need to do a right bit of tradin'"
Anonymous

Marketing

Marketing / Tradin'

If you're learning to build as a hobby, this chapter is just a bunch of words. For those who wish to turn this into a living, this chapter is designed to help you sell your furniture. We have learned some very valuable lessons from costly mistakes. We hope this chapter will minimize your mistakes and better your chances at succeeding in this craft. Our first suggestion would be to concentrate on your strengths and recognize your possible weaknesses, we are carpenters and craftsmen not salesmen or marketing specialist. Listening to others who are and a willingness too learn, will greatly increase the success of your efforts. Secondly, we suggest you "Barnumize" your business. If you don't know what that means then we strongly suggest that you get a copy of "There's a Customer Born Every Minute" by Joe Vitale and read it cover to cover. You will soon discover Branum was so much more than a circus owner and promoter. We have completely Barnumized our business and if you want an easier road to success, so will you.

Our independence and freedom has always been our principal motivating factor in business. We work with the greatest looking lumber mother nature has to offer, and do what we enjoy, that makes all the difference in the world to us. Every piece of furniture we build is unique in it's own way, and that in itself seems to keep every day new and challenging. In spring and summer we build garden swings, flower boxes and other outdoor furniture. In the fall and winter, we build more interior pieces, beds, dressers, coffee tables, nightstands, etc. It's a fantastic way to earn a living,!

Still no matter how far we think we've escaped from corporate life, we still have to get our product to market. In the beginning, the first pieces built will not be your best. It's important to keep a sense of humor with those first pieces and not get discouraged. Sell at a discount or give those first pieces to friends and family. When we look back at some pictures of the first things we've built it is a very humbling experience. But, at the same time, we see how much we've learned and how much better our furniture is today. Customers will pay top dollar, but they want top quality craftsmanship. Solid joinery, creativity, functionality and the finish are all important confidence builders for your customers. Customers have so many choices of builders and styles, your furniture must stand out. Build it right and you can offer a lifetime guarantee. Now, you're ready for marketing you goods.

Selling through Classified Ads

Sell pieces through the classified ad section of your newspaper. Place an ad like the example below. In fact, this is how Les started our company. He built a bunk bed, didn't really like it and ended up selling five or six of them. Before he knew it, he was doing referral business from word of mouth. Place an ad in the furniture section of the classifieds, and see if anyone responds.

> Pine log furniture for sale.
> Queen size bed $750.
> Pine & Aspen nightstands $150 ea.
> 555-5555

Selling on Consignment

Consignment is a low risk way for your log furniture to get into local furniture and speciality stores. You will also gain valued experience working with retailers. Consignment means you get paid when the furniture sells, thus the store owner is more likely to take the risk with his floor space and display your furniture. We suggest you start with placing one or two of your best pieces in a retailers store then add more based on your furniture sales performance as well as the type of referrals you may have received. Negotiate a fair wholesale price for your furniture. Different than the classified ad approach, you will be splitting the sale price with your retailers. Most Consignment fees range from forty to sixty percent to the retailer. When you are starting out, any and all sales are good sales. Be flexible with your prices. Over time you can educate your retailers why doweling your furniture will last for generations and that each piece is hand crafted, hand sanded and hand finished. Challenge them to compare structural integrity with factory furniture. Are you really comparing apples to apples? Building the value and educating retailers and their staff will end up benefiting everyone and ultimately you can raise your prices a bit. Your furniture needs to be in front of the customer before they can buy it. Spend the winter with barn full of furniture and it won't do anyone any good.

Marketing & Advertising Materials

In order for a product to sell, buyers need to know what you have and lugging furniture samples everywhere you go can be somewhat cumbersome. We suggest creating a brochure, flyer, or even a small catalog that will display your craft in a pleasing manner. Start by taking pictures of the furniture and accessories you build. Select the best photos and then describe in a text area special features and benefits as well as a brief description of each piece. Now you're ready for what a designer calls the layout. If you have one or two items you will do fine with a flyer or two. If you have several varieties of items you may want something larger like a brochure. A professional graphic designer can help layout and produce the best marketing options for your product and your budget. Once completed, the retailers with whom you consign will use these tools to sell your furniture to customers; you will use them to give to potential retailers, and your customers.

Our first brochure was a simple black and white photo copied layout which was folded into thirds. It gave a brief description about our company, and our approach to building quality handcrafted log furniture. It listed our company name, address and phone number. You can even include a picture of yourself adding a personal touch. A business card is ok, but a few pictures of your furniture is better.

Flea Markets and Trade Shows

Gather a sampling of furniture and accessories that reflect what you enjoy building and rent a booth at a near by flea market or trade show. This is a great way to introduce you and your furniture to potential new customers. Years ago during the summer months, our sales manager sold mexican rustic furniture at flea markets across the country and made a good living. It's a gypsy lifestyle, but if you like to travel and have a way to haul your furniture, you can make enough in summer to last through the winter. Here in Colorado, it is not unusual to see a roadside stand selling log furniture. This type of marketing seems to bring out the bargain hunter. Factory made bar stools are frequently sold for less than twenty dollars. If you build quality furniture with character it will bring much more.

The Internet

This newer medium is changing our market and brings crafters like us almost endless new possibilities. Connecting crafters, retailers and consumers this new marketing tool can help develop your business. Unlike the photo copied brochure we started with, people anywhere in the world can look up our web site at www.Bestlogfurniture.net There, interested folks can find out more about our products and services. They can print pictures and information with just a click of a button. In this case our brochure was printed at their house on their paper without us investing in postage or printing cost. The possibilities of the web are endless. Who knows, maybe someday people will visit your virtual showroom. In any case, a presence on the internet is important and can generate sales for your business.

Traditional Advertising

Business directories, yellow pages, magazines, billboards, radio ads, and television are just a few examples of traditional advertising. Though these types of marketing have varying degrees of success they can be expensive. Investigate the costs in your area then see if they fit your marketing budget. On several occasions we have been able to barter advertising in exchange for services. The payment of the design and printing of our first color brochure included a rustic 10ft. ladder which made the project more affordable for us.

Your Own Retail Shop

If your small sales ventures have been successful and you love the process of owning your own business this could become your dream. If so we wish you the best. The opportunity for you to receive the full retail price for your furniture and experience the pleasure of numerous satisfied customers has its own rewards. However, there are many considerations to take in to account. You will need to consider supply and demand issues for your product, the local economy, location, and staffing a small furniture shop, to name a few.

Our company's goal has been to help connect crafters as store owners with other crafters that can supply your store with items you don't build. This gives your store a better inventory and the other crafter another retail outlet. This type of networking will strengthen the industry and bring a positive economic end to all our efforts.

Each crafter has a different talent and look to their pieces. All the different looks and styles ensures potential customers a great selection to choose from. One customer may like a real rustic look, while the other might prefer a real clean look.

It is important to work with other crafters; our business has grown because of our willingness to work with other builders. Besides, one or even two builders could not build all the furniture we sell. The only factory capable of mass production is the human factory. No matter how big the advances in technology, it can not replace real artistic creativity and craftsmanship. Learn the trade, and not just the tricks of the trade. One of a kind furniture built with integrity will always have a market.

This book and accompanying video are proof this industry is constantly changing. We have taught hundreds of students, thus helping us recognize the need for this information. We know that almost anyone is capable of building their own log furniture, with all different kinds of tools and techniques. We know we can build only so much furniture in our lifetime. Our efforts to share what we know will simply give us a better chance of maintaining the opportunity to build and sell our furniture and make a living. The more of you who join us the merrier.

Ten Projects You Can Build

Tip:

We suggest those who are just beginning to build furniture start with project 8, the dinning chair. Building this log chair will help to familiarize you with several aspects of log crafting. These skills will be used again and again as you learn to "Build Your Own Log Furniture"

5.1 Step Stool

*N*o house is complete without a good footstool. Kids needing to brush their teeth can't reach the faucet, and everybody that needs to tie a shoe or reach up to that top shelf in the closet needs a footstool. This is the easiest project to build as a beginner. To last all the years of people standing and setting on the bench, you need to use healthy wood and make sure all the joints are strong.

CUT LIST

1 Top piece	2-3" inches thick
	12-14 inches wide
	14-18 inches long
4 Legs	2-3 inches in diameter
	Cut all four legs 13 inches long.
4 Dowels	3/8 inch dowel
	4-5 inches long

STEP 1.

On the underside of the top piece, mark the spot you want to drill the four holes or mortise for the legs. Use a tape measure and measure in 2 inches from each corner and put a mark.

STEP 2.

Using a 1 1/2" forstner / saw tooth bit, drill the four holes a full 1 1/2" deep. To give the legs a slight angle out, stand over the top piece, place the bit on your mark and start drilling as soon as the bit starts to take, lean the drill towards you angling in line with the corner. This angle is roughly 8 – 10 degrees.

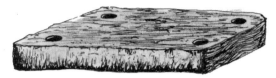

STEP 3.

Put a 1 1/2 inch diameter tenon, 1 1/2 inch long, on all four legs. Do not angle your tenons. Drill in line with the other end so your tenons are as straight as possible.

STEP 4.

Place glue in the mortise/hole, and place some glue on each tenon. Put the legs into the bench and spin/twist until each tenon is all the way in the mortise for a snug fit.

STEP 5.

Set the stool right side up and see how it stands. Look at the angle of the legs to see if they match each other. Spin or twist the legs to adjust their direction.

STEP 6.

With the angle of the legs the way you want them, it's time to dowel them into place. For this you'll need a 3/8 inch auger bit and the four dowel pieces you cut earlier. Review the chapter on doweling for more detailed instructions. The dowels should be drilled as the example below shows.

STEP 7.

Place glue on both the dowel and in the dowel hole. Pound in the dowels until you hear a deep sound or thud. This tells you your dowel is all the way in.

STEP 8.

Cut off or grind down the exposed or extra dowel.

STEP 9.

If the stool legs are not the same lengths, you need to level up the legs. Grind or cut down the legs until the stool fits flat and stable on all four legs, and sets level.

STEP 10.

Round off the edges, sand the stool and your ready to apply a finish. (See Finishes page 57)

The coat rack is a staple in any cabin, home or hideaway. This project is quite simple, making it a great beginning project. If you can successfully hang your hat, scarf or coat, this project will be a success. Use your creativity and imagination. Build something that is pleasing to <u>your</u> eye.

The illustration shows a half log coat rack with three hooks. Use whatever materials you have on hand. We built a series of coat racks using fence posts and railroad spikes, as well as old rusty horseshoes for hooks. On one of the racks, we tacked some old barbwire across the top for authenticity. One family brought us a piece of wood from a cabin their grandfather had built and asked us to make a small coat rack as a tribute and reminder to use in their new cabin. That coat rack is a real treasure for their family.

To build a coat rack like the one illustrated, follow this cut list: For a longer or bigger coat rack, cut a longer half log piece and cut more hooks.

Evenly space your hooks at least six inches apart. Hooks are typically 7 inches long. This length allows for a 1 to 1 1/2" long tenon.

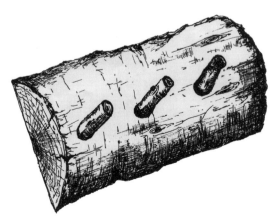

CUT LIST

One half log 21 inches long.

Splitting a log in half can be done as illustrated. Using a hammer and wedge split a short log in half. If you have a big band saw rip what you need in just a few minutes.

3 Hooks
      7 1/2 inches long
      1 inch in diameter.

STEP 1.

Round all edges and corners of the half log piece. This is a good time to use your Angle Grinder with a 36 grit disk. Sand and smooth with your sander using 80 grit sandpaper.

STEP 2.

Cut three hook pieces you cut and put a 1 inch diameter tenon, 1 to 1 1/2 inches long on one end of all three hooks. (See tenons page 43)

Typically, make all the tenons 1 1/2 inches long, however in this case the thickness of your half log piece dictates the length of tenon to be used. Grind and sand these pieces.

STEP 3.

Using a tape measure, measure in from both ends 3 1/2 inches and make a mark.

STEP 4.

From one end, measure in 10 1/2 inches and make a mark. These three marks should equally lay out the hooks for the coat rack. There should be six inches between hooks.

STEP 5.

Using a 1 inch forstner or paddle bit, drill the three holes (Mortise) for each hook. It is important to match the drill bit to the diame-

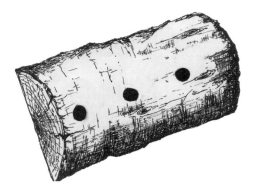

ter of the tenon. Drill three holes with a slight angle. The hook should angle up about 5 degrees or so. This will keep whatever is hung on it from slipping off.

STEP 6.

Glue hooks into holes and spin or twist into place. Glue both surfaces.

STEP 7.

Using a 1 1/2 inch wood screw, from the back of the half log piece and directly behind each hook, run a single wood screw for added support. This will add to the strength of the hooks.

STEP 8.

Check for any glue spots and remove excess glue and give a final sand, Your ready to put on a finish. (See Finishes page 57)

Bar stools are typically 29 inches tall. Too tall and it might have a tendency to tip over, too short and you will feel like a little kid setting at your bar. You can always adjust the dimensions below to better suite your needs.

CUT LIST

For the purpose of this book we are going to illustrate using a 2-inch thick top or seat.

One Seat/top piece	15 inches diameter 2 inches thick.
4 Legs@	30 inches long (2 1/2 - 3 inch diameter)
2 Rungs@	14 inches long (2 inch diameter)
2 Rungs @	15 1/2 inches long (2 inch diameter)
2 Rungs@	20 inches long (2 inch diameter)
2 Rungs@	21 1/2 inches long 1 2 inch diameter)

STEP 1.

Follow the cut list and mark all your pieces.

STEP 2.

Peel and sand your pieces.

STEP 3.

Place tenons on the following pieces. *We recommend a 1 1/2-inch diameter tenon, 1 1/2-inches long.*

All four legs get one tenon on the smallest end.

All 8 rungs get a tenon on both ends.

STEP 4.

Measure up from the bottom of each leg 4 1/2 inches and make a mark.

STEP 5.

Using a 1 1/2 inch forstner or saw tooth bit, drill a 1 1/2-inch deep mortise (hole). in each leg.

STEP 6.

We are building the two sides (See illustration above), - So, in line with the last holes you made in steps 4 and 5, measure up 18 inches from the bottom and make a mark.

STEP 7.

Using a 1 1/2-inch forstner or saw tooth bit, drill a 1 1/2-inch deep mortise. Again, one hole in each leg.

STEP 8.

Take two legs, one 14-inch rung and one 20-inch rung, glue and dowel. (see doweling page 47) Repeat to build the other side.

STEP 9.

With your seat bottom side up on your workbench, find and mark where to drill holes for the legs.

Drill these holes using the same 1 1/2-inch bit. Notice the legs have about a 10 degree angle. Once you start your drill. Lean the drill to compensate for this angle. Remember practice makes perfect and keep a sense of humor. This may take a few tries.

STEP 10.

Place the two sides into the seat (**Do not glue**).

This is a dry assembly. When you have the stool in the position you want, and all the angles look the same, determine where to drill for the rungs that will tie this stool together.

STEP 11.

The tie in rungs should go just above the other rung. The reason they are just above the other rungs, is that the tenons should not intersect. By raising this last tie in rung, you will miss the adjacent rung and its tenon.

If your logs are bent, or you are using a larger or smaller diameter log, you may have to adjust the length of the tie in rungs. The goal is to have the angle of all four legs the same.

STEP 12.

Glue and dowel all remaining mortise and tenon joints. Glue and dowel legs to the seat. Cut off excess dowel and sand any rough spots. Let stand and dry.

STEP 13.

You are not done, the order was for six bar stools. So what are you waiting for? Repeat steps 1-12, five more times.

STEP 14.

Now you're ready to apply a finish. (see Finishing page 57)

5.4 Ladder

$\mathcal{B}$uild ladders of all sizes for all types of uses. Ladders accent a room, and sometimes are used to display blankets, etc. They are also used to access lofts, libraries and bunk beds. Pine is strong and is typically the material used.

Building ladders is great practice for making tenons and doweling.

CUT LIST

For the purpose of this example we will outline a 6-foot ladder.

2 @ 72inches Side posts
(3inch diameter)

7 @ 15 inches Rungs
(2-2 1/2 inch diameter)

STEP 1.

Follow the cut list and cut all your pieces.

STEP 2.

Put a 1-1/2" diameter tenon 1 1/2" long on both ends of the 7 rungs.

STEP 3.

Time to drill the mortise (holes) in the side posts. Lying them flat on the ground next to each other. Using your tape measure and a good black marker, mark the following measurements and drill holes 1 1/2 inches deep.

9"

18"

27"

36"

45"

54"

63"

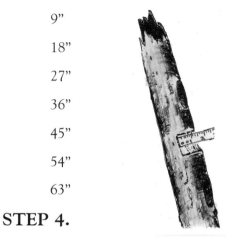

STEP 4.

Drawknife, grind and sand all your pieces.

STEP 5.

Glue your ladder together. Remember to put glue on both surfaces and twist or spin the rung(s) to get all 7 in place.

STEP 6.

Now that the ladder is glued, pick up the ladder and drop it on each side a couple times or pound on the sides with a rubber mallet. This will force the tenons into the mortise for a real snug fit.

STEP 7.

Using a 3/8-inch auger bit and 14 pieces of dowel 5 inches long, dowel the rungs into place.

(See Doweling page 47)

STEP 8.

Cut of any excess dowel and sand smooth. Check over the ladder for other glue spots you can clean up with the sander.

STEP 9.

Allow glue to dry, and your ready to apply a finish. (See Finishes)

*N*o rustic living room is complete without a coffee table. Coffee tables come in all different sizes and styles. The most challenging aspect of this project is building the top. (See making tops page 53) If you can build good tops for coffee tables, you're well on your way to building dinning tables, dressers and more.

All throughout this book, we have emphasized using your own creativity and to build what is pleasing to your eye. This project will help you focus on your own judgement, creativity and style.

Typically a coffee table is 15 to 17 inches tall, 24 inches wide and 48 inches long. That is the entire dimensions and cut list information you are going to get for this project. It's time you figured one out for yourself. Provided you have built a couple of other projects in this book you should not have too much trouble determining what to do. If you are a beginner, consider building a chair and a nightstand before the coffee table.

The illustrations show two types of coffee tables. The first is a coffee table with a four-way wrap. You can see the four logs connected to the legs. These logs give the table cross support (side to side & front to back). This design is very sturdy.

The illustration below shows a crisscross support. One cross support is higher and one is lower. In the center, where the supports meet, they are doweled together. This design allows your guests to have more legroom around the table and easier access with the vacuum.

Still other coffee tables have a lower shelf for magazines, etc. See photo at the beginning of this project on page 91. To learn how to build a lower shelf for your coffee table, see nightstands section 5.7 on page 99.

Take notes regarding the cuts you make, and when someone asks you to build them a coffee table, you will be able to duplicate it without much difficulty.

STEP 1.

Build your top.

The size of your top will dictate the rest of the pieces with the exception of the height. Obviously, the height will be determined by the length of the table legs combined with the thickness of your top.

If you have any questions, see making tops page 53.

STEP 2.

Cut four legs to the desired length. The diameter of the logs is up to you.

STEP 3.

Decide how you are going to attach the legs to the top. (See attaching legs page 55)

STEP 4.

Decide what type of cross support you will use. Four way wrap, crisscross, lower shelf or a totally different design all your own

Cut the pieces to rough lengths.

STEP 5.

Peel, grind and sand the pieces to the finish look you desire.

STEP 6.

Attach the four legs to the top, but don't tighten all the way or glue just yet.

STEP 7.

Measure and mark where the cross supports should go.

STEP 8.

Drill holes (Mortise).

STEP 9.

Place tenons on the cross support pieces.

STEP 10.

Insert cross supports into mortise

Ensure everything is level and your legs are either at a pleasing angle or straight up and down.

STEP 11.

Glue and dowel all joints, and tighten fully the legs to the top.

STEP 12.

Check the piece over for any rough spots, or glue drips. Give a final sanding and your ready to put on a finish. (See finishing page 57).

Notes:

_____

_____

_____

_____

_____

_____

_____

_____

Your Drawing

5.6 Rustic Toy Box

This project is really the start of making case goods (dressers, desks, armoires, etc.). Dan's grandfather was a master cabinet builder in the Ohio valley. He once told him, that "Making cabinets (dressers) is simply building boxes. Build good boxes and you'll build good cabinets". What better place to start than a rustic toy box. Build this box from cedar and it is a great blanket box for Grandma's quilts!! The moths will hate it?

We call it rustic to explain the mistakes we make. Real rustic just means it's supposed to look that way. It is why we don't call it fine log furnishings. You will get significantly better with each one you build (or less rustic).

The toy box dimensions will be 24 X 24 X 24. No latch or hinges on this toy box, the lid is either on or off.

For this project you will need to obtain 36 ft of 1 X 10-inch pine board. These are normally sold in six-foot lengths. Six, six footers should do ya. You will also need a small sheet of quarter inch plywood for the bottom of the toy box and a handful of 1 1/2 inch wood screws or nails and a handful of one inch wood screws or nails.

You also need a 10-inch handle for the top. Try to pick a piece with some character. (see making handles page 51)

CUT LIST

12 Side and End pieces@   23" long
1" X 10" stock
(rip on table saw to 8 inches)

3 Top pieces@   25" inches long
1" X 10" stock
(rip on table saw to 8 inches)

2 cleats or cleating @   21 inches
(Rip on the table saw
into one-inch strips)

2 cleats or cleating @   24 inches
(Rip on the table saw
into one-inch strips)

1 bottom piece of quarter inch plywood
23 7/8 inches X 23 7/8 inches square.

1 Gnarly handel piece

STEP 1.

Follow the cut list and prepare pieces.

STEP 2.

Look at the illustration below, as it is an overview of this project. Notice the cleats on the side and end pieces. Look closer and see the cleats on the side pieces are inset 1-1/2 inches. This allows for the box to fit together flush and square on all corners.

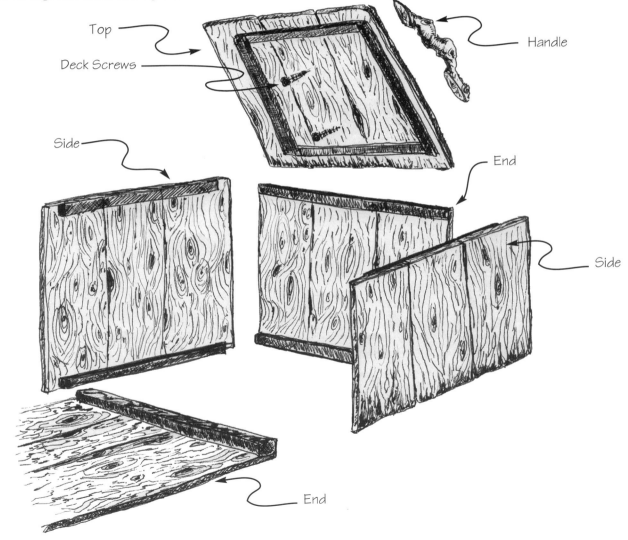

Top

Deck Screws

Handle

Side

End

Side

End

STEP 3.

Using three 23 inch long 1 X 8 inch boards, and two cleats 21 inches long, build one side of the box. Lay the three pieces flat on your work bench glue and screw the cleat to side pieces. Leave 1-1/2 inches on either side of the cleat. Repeat to build the other side. Use a framing square to square up your pieces. Or you can trace the square lines on the top of the bench and match the pieces up to the lines.

STEP 4.

Using three 23 inch long 1 X 8 inch boards, and two cleats 24 inches long, build one end of the toy box. The cleating should be flush with the end of the boards. Square up the boards and glue and screw the cleating to the boards. Repeat to build the other side.

STEP 5.

Connect the side and end pieces, in other words, time to frame out the box. Glue and screw each of the four corners together.

STEP 6.

Take the three 25 inch top pieces and place them together on the floor. Place the box on top of the three pieces and square the box as best you can with the top pieces. Take your pencil and trace the inside of the box. This will show you where to place the cleating for the top of the toy box. Go ahead and assemble the top of the box, using the left over cleating.

STEP 7.

We are going to put the bottom of the toy box in. Start by putting glue on the top of the bottom cleats on the inside of the box. Slide down and in the plywood and center it on the cleating the best you can. Attach with 1-inch wood screws.

STEP 8.

Attach top handle with glue and wood screws, and your done. Check the whole piece over for any sharp points and rough edges and sand them down. You are ready to apply the finish. (see Finishes page 57)

5.7 Night Stand & End Table

For the purpose of building, we are going to walk you through a nightstand. An end table is basically the same, with a few exceptions. Typically end tables are longer to provide space for a lamp and lower to match the height of the couch.

The height of a nightstand should be 1-2 inches lower than the mattress of the bed or what we call bed height. As a standard, we build a 20" X 20" top. The top material is 1-2 inches thick. (See Making Tops)

Obviously, build yours to suite the dimensions you want. Use your own creativity and modify these plans to fit your design.

CUT LIST

4 @ 27"   Legs (2-3 inches in diameter)

2 @ 15"   Rungs or crosspieces for bottom shelf (1–2 inches in diameter)

Top Material for 20" X 20" top (4 board's 20 inches long, 5 inches wide, 1-2 inches thick)

Material for bottom shelf (3 boards 20 inches long, 5 inches wide, 1-2 inches thick

STEP 1.

Follow the cut list and cut all your pieces.

STEP 2.

Make your top. (see Building Tops page 53).

STEP 3.

Put 1 1/2 " tenons on both ends of both 15" Rungs (crosspieces).

STEP 4.

Drawknife and sand the four legs.

STEP 5.

Drawknife and sand the two rungs (crosspieces).

STEP 6.

Measure up from the bottom of each leg 6" and make a mark. Using a 1 1/2" Saw Tooth Forstner bit, drill a mortise (hole) 1 1/2" deep. One mortise per leg.

STEP 7.

Fit one of the rungs into the mortise of two of the legs, glue and dowel together. See illustration below.

STEP 8.

Repeat step 7 with the remaining two legs .

🎋 Tip; place this second pieces on top of the set you assembled in step 7 and build to match. *Matching both sides visually and proportionally will enhance the over all look of the piece.*

STEP 9.

Attach the legs to the top. (see attaching legs page 55). Pick the technique that best works for the tools you have on hand.

STEP 10.

It's time to build the bottom shelf. This shelf will tie the piece together and give the night stand side to side strength.

Fitting Pieces

Start by laying the three boards across the two rungs. Make any leveling adjustments necessary **Before** you attach the shelf pieces, If you are using twisted or gnarled logs, they may need to be cut, sanded or ground down any high points that keep the shelf from setting level.

Attaching Shelf

There are several ways to attach the shelf pieces. We think we should list a few ways and show them how to do at least one way. You can dowel the shelf in place, or drill a 3/8 inch countersink, insert deck screw and cap the hole with a small piece of 3/8 inch doweling. Grind off excess and sand smooth.

You can also use more than the three boards we've suggested. Come up with your own design. If you're building a taller nightstand, you might consider adding a second shelf.

STEP 11.

Check the nightstand for level by placing it on a flat level surface. Make any adjustments that might be necessary.

STEP 12.

Check the nightstand over for any glue, round all your corners and do a final sanding. Allow time for the glue to dry and your ready to put on a finish. (see Finishing page 57).

5.8 Dinning Chair

Typically, chairs are built from pine. Considered a softwood, pine is stronger than aspen. Chairs take a lot of abuse over the years, so they need to be durable. For instance, aspen dents or marks easier than pine. Built correctly, this chair will last for generations.

Use your creativity, as the spindles in the back rest area need to have some character to them. Build a half dozen of them before you judge your work too harshly. If you don't like this design, create your own, or even a combination of the two. The seat material can be barn wood, rough sawn lumber, or some old 2 X 4 scrap.

CUT LIST

Recommended log diameter is:
$2^1/2$ - 3 inches.

2	@ 40" --------------	Back legs
2	@ 18" --------------	Front legs
5	@ $14^1/2$" ----------	Cross pieces
2	@ 14" --------------	Side pieces
1	@ 19" --------------	Top cross
2	@ 17" --------------	Back spindles

Use 13/4" diameter logs

3 Pieces of seat material 1-$1^1/2$" thick,
7–8" wide and $19^1/2$"–20" long

19, $3/8$" dowels roughly 4" long

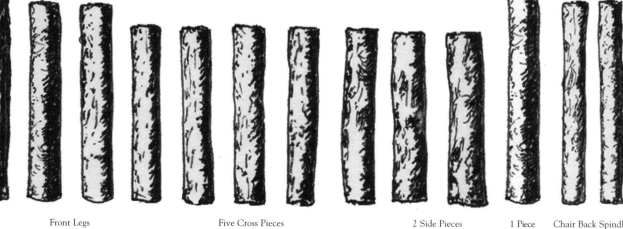

Chair Back & legs
40"

Front Legs
18"

Five Cross Pieces
(Rungs)
$14^1/2$"

2 Side Pieces
(Rungs)
14"

1 Piece
19"

Chair Back Spindles
17"

STEP 1.

Cut the pieces according to the cut list, which is provided. Mark all of the pieces with a marker for ease in identification latter.

STEP 2.

After your logs have been cut to length, put tenons on the following pieces as listed below.

We recommend a $1^1/2$" diameter tenon that is $1^1/2$" long.

TENONS

Each 18" front leg piece gets one tenon on the smallest end.

All 5 of the $14^1/2$" rung cross pieces get tenons on both ends.

Each 14" rung piece gets tenons on both ends.

Put a tenon on one end of both spindles.

Front Legs
18"
*One tenon on smallest end
of each post.*

Five Cross Pieces
(Rungs)
$14^1/2$"

2 Side Pieces
(Rungs)
14"

Chair Back Spindles
17"

STEP 3.

Drawknife, grind and sand all the pieces. It is much easier to prep each piece now, while you can individually handle them. Choose the type of finished look, whether it is clean with no bark, a skip peel, or a bark on look. (see Finishes page 57).

STEP 4.

Now that you ar probably tired of grinding and sanding, it is time to drill the holes and start the assembly of the chair. First, you will to build the back section of the chair.

Starting from the small end of the 40" pieces, measure down and put a mark at 2" / 18" / 22 $1/2$"/ and 32".

Using a $1^1/2$" saw tooth/forstner bit, dill your holes $1^1/2$" deep. Some people drill these holes with a drill press,but we just lie them flat on the floor and drill. Point the drill straight up and down, as you do not want to drill at an angle.

Back Spindles

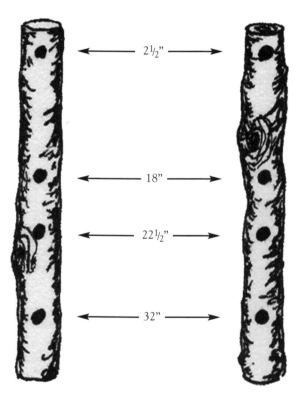

STEP 5.

Time to assemble the back of the chair. Follow the diagram below. For a great bond, apply glue to both surfaces of the tenon and mortise.

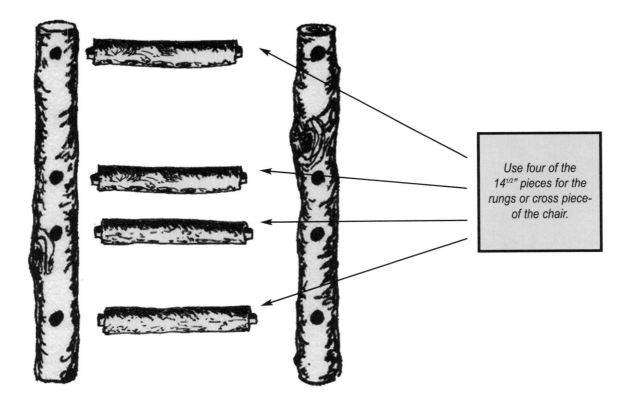

Use four of the 14$^{1/2}$" pieces for the rungs or cross piece of the chair.

🐝 **Note,** You may have to twist or spin the rungs to line up with the holes. Once each rung is in place, pound on the side of the posts with a rubber hammer to set or drive the tenons in for a snug fit.

STEP 6.

Lay the piece flat on the floor to see there is no twist or warp. If necessary, wrestle or twist until the entire section lies flat to the surface. This is shown in greater detail in the video.

STEP 7.

Using your $1^1/2$" forstner bit, we are going to drill holes for the spindles. Drill the bottom hole $1^1/2$" deep. Drill the top hole $1^1/2$" deep.

STEP 8.

To measure the length of your spindles see the diagram below. You are measuring from inside the top hole, down to the surface or top of the bottom rung.

Measure this distance and divide into thirds. Drill spindle holes. (see step 7)

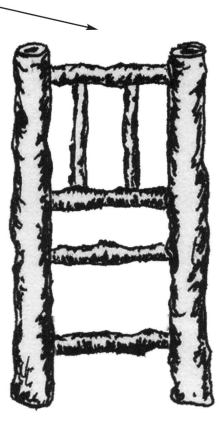

STEP 9.

Using the two 17" spindle pieces $1^3/4$" in diameter. You should already have a tenon on one end. This tenon will go in the top hole. From the tip of the tenon measure and cut to length.

Put a short $1/2$" tenon on the bottom end of the spindle. Apply glue and slid in the top tenon, and drop down the bottom tenon into the hole. Again you may need to spin or twist the spindle to line it up. This procedure is covered in the video.

Step 10.

With the back section of the chair built, it is time to build the front section of the chair.

Take the two 18" pieces (the front legs), and measure from the bottom up 8" and make a mark, (see diagram below). Using your $1^{1/2}$ forstner bit, drill holes $1^{1/2}$ deep. Take a $14^{1/2}$ crosspiece and glue into place. Once together, lie the section flat on the floor and proceed to the next step.

STEP 11.

Take the 19" log piece (the one with NO TENONS) and position it as shown in the diagram below. Mark, drill, glue and assemble.

8"

STEP 12.

With both front and back sections assembled, it's time to tie the chair together. Lay both pieces on the floor as shown below.

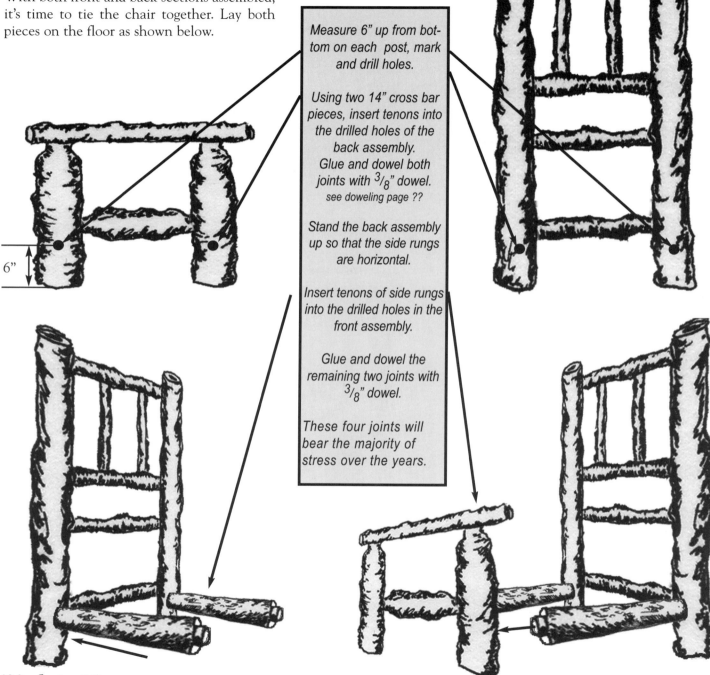

Measure 6" up from bottom on each post, mark and drill holes.

Using two 14" cross bar pieces, insert tenons into the drilled holes of the back assembly.
Glue and dowel both joints with $3/8$" dowel.
see doweling page ??

Stand the back assembly up so that the side rungs are horizontal.

Insert tenons of side rungs into the drilled holes in the front assembly.

Glue and dowel the remaining two joints with $3/8$" dowel.

These four joints will bear the majority of stress over the years.

6"

STEP 13.

Using the three seat pieces or what ever seat materials you have and cut out with a jigsaw or whatever tool you have to do the job– one for the left side and one for the right. Set in

place, take the third piece and cut to fit. Grind and sand all three pieces.

STEP 15.

Grind down dowels and sand smooth. Check the rest of the chair for glue spots and any ruff spots and sand. You're now ready to apply a finish coat to your chair. (see Finishes page 57).

STEP 14.

Set pieces into position and attach to chair using $^3/8$" dowels.

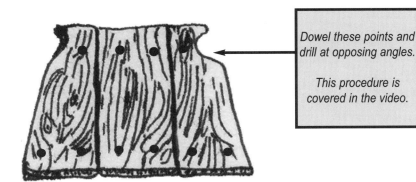

Dowel these points and drill at opposing angles.

This procedure is covered in the video.

5.9 Beds

TWIN SIZE   39 1/2" X 75"
    Cut bed rails   81" long

FULL SIZE   54" X 75"
    Cut bed rails   81" long

QUEEN SIZE   60" X 80"
    Cut bed rails   86" long

KING SIZE   76" X 80"
    Cut bed rails   86" long

Before building any log bed there are a few things the builder needs to know.

1. What size bed
2. What type of wood i.e.: Aspen or Pine, or other soft woods you have access to.
3. Spindle configuration (Straight up and down, or flared out) or your own design.
4. Thickness of both box spring and mattress combined.
5. Desired bed height (From floor to the top of the mattress).
6. Height of headboard and footboard posts (Typically 60 inches for the headboard, and 40 inches for the footboard.
7. What type of finish (light/Dark, Oil/flat or urethane/gloss).

Note, *for the sake of illustration we are going to use queen bed measurements*

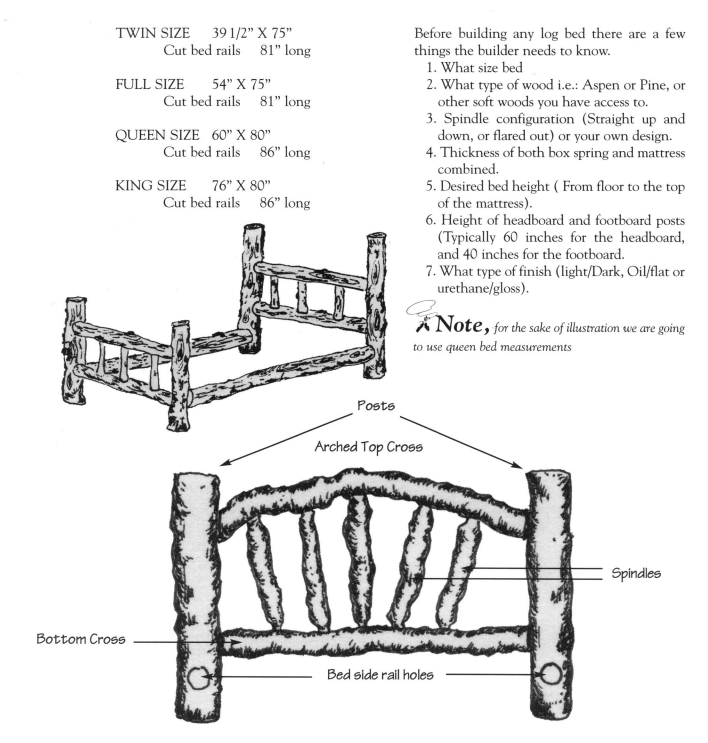

Posts

Arched Top Cross

Spindles

Bottom Cross

Bed side rail holes

STEP 1.

Cut logs to length, peel and sand all 4 posts. Two headboard posts 60 inches and two footboard posts 40 inches.

STEP 2.

Using one nail or screw for each post and two 2X4 Jigs attach a jig to the top and bottom of the bed posts as shown below. This will temporarily hold the posts at the proper width (60 inches for a queen bed) and allow the post to turn for mortise drilling access.

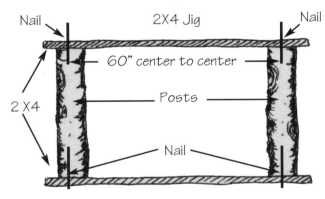

Tip: Laying your posts on the ground works best for this process. The photo below illustrates how the jig and posts will appear when you have completed this step.

STEP 3.

Select 4 cross pieces and rough cut them to 70 inches. Refer to the illustration on the previous page.

 If this is your first bed, we suggest you pick straight logs to use as your cross pieces. However, you are the designer/builder and know your specific skill level.

STEP 4.

Mark the desired bed height on the Headboard Posts. This measurement represents how high the top of the Mattress is from the floor.

Next, locate the side rail mortise placement on headboard posts. **Do not drill at this time.** To locate mortise placement measure down from your bed height the thickness of both the mattress and the box spring combined plus 2 inches. *In this example the mattress and box spring combined thickness is 16 inches so our mark is at 18 inches.*

Measure from the center of the side rail mortise mark on the headboard post, down to the bottom of the posts. (In the example shown, it is 7 inches). This is the measurement you will use to mark the side rail mortise on the footboard posts.

Tip: When marking the posts of the head board ensure the bottom cross piece placement is higher or lower than your side rails placement, the tenons of each must not intersect.

STEP 5.

Lay the bottom Cross Piece on top of the two headboard posts. The top of the cross piece should be 2 inches above the bed height marks. This piece should show when the mattress is on the bed, if it is too high the pillows will fall down behind the bed.

Lay the top cross piece on top of headboard posts at the height you want. There is no real guideline for how high you set this piece. We suggest 4-6 inches down from the top of your posts.

STEP 6.

Measure between the posts, inside to inside, and add two inches on each end for the 2 inch tenons Mark your cross pieces to length.
Mark the mortise placement for your cross pieces, spin or turn the post and drill mortise.

STEP 7.

Ratchet strap the cross pieces to a saw horse.

Remember to drill tenons straight.

Tenons follow an imaginary straight line, and do not follow the curve of the cross piece.

Using a 2 5/8 inch Dowel Plug Cutter w/ half inch drive drill put put a 2inch tenons on each end of the cross pieces.

Cut off outer ring to expose the tenon. This can be done several ways. Chain saw, drawknife,, hand saw, or chisel and hammer.

STEP 8. Turn post so markings are facing up. Using a 2 5/8 inch Forstner bit with half inch drive drill, hold drill straight up and down and drill the four holes for the cross pieces at the marks you made on the posts.

STEP 9.

Remove the 2x4 jigs. Dry assemble cross pieces into posts and ratchet tight. Check that your posts are in line with each other.

Top View
looking down on Posts.

Right Way:

Imaginary straight line

Wrong Way:

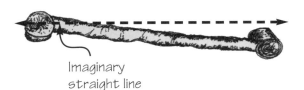

Imaginary
straight line

Note: You may have to wrestle with the piece to straighten it out. Also be sure to have the tenons all the way into the hole for a snug fit.

STEP 10.

Spindles. Be sure to place the spindles close enough together to maintain back support. You don't want to fall through the back and hit the wall. The diameter of your spindles should be 3-5". Generally we do the following spindle count.

Twins

    3 Spindles in headboard and
    3 in the foot boards.

Full/Double

    5 Spindles in head board and
    3 in foot board.

Queen

    5 to 7 in Headboard and
    3 to 5 in foot boards.

King

    7 to 9 in headboard
    4 to 7 in footboard.

Find the center of both cross pieces and make a mark. Using the center as a guide, mark where you want your spindles from the center out to posts.

STEP 11.

Loosen ratchet and turn crosspieces so that markings are facing up for drilling. Using a 1 and a half inch forstner bit with half inch drive drill, drill the holes for the spindles. Top holes 1 1/2 inches deep, bottom holes **1/2 inch** deep.

After drilling, turn (spin) the crosspiece back so the holes are facing each other. Using your tape, measure from inside the spindle mortise of the top cross piece to the surface of the spindle mortise in the bottom cross piece. (see illustration below)

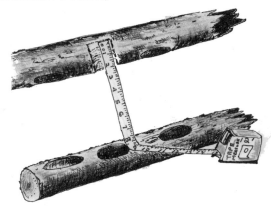

STEP 12.

Mark the spindles and cut to length. Using your 1 1/2 inch tenon cutter, put a full 1 1/2 inch tenon on one end, but only a **1/2 inch** tenon on the other end. Repeat this process with all tenons. (We show this technique in our video)

STEP 13.

Insert the long top tenons into the mortise spaces in the top cross piece, slide up and drop the short tenon down in the mortise spaces of the bottom cross piece. (*You may have to spin or turn the spindle to line up the tenon with the bottom mortise.*)

STEP 14.

Once all your spindles are cut and fit into place, peel and sand them. Dry assemble the headboard/footboard and ratchet tight and re check for proper alignment as shown in step 9.

STEP 15.

Once the headboard/footboard is aligned properly, loosen ratchet. Work quickly to glue all tenon and mortise joints. Once all joints are glued check the alignment and tighten ratchet again. (see step 9)

STEP 16.

Using a 3/8 inch auger bit with a 3/8 inch dowel, first dowel the bottom of each spindle to the bottom cross piece, applying glue to both dowel and hole surfaces. Next dowel the top of each spindle to the top cross piece again apply glue to both dowel and hole surfaces. (see doweling page 57).

STEP 17.

Dowel the cross pieces to the bed posts, using a 5/8 inch auger bit with a 5/8 inch dowel. Glue dowel and hole to ensure a good bond. Once the dowels are in, sand down the excess dowel with your grinder so the dowel is flush with the surface of the log. (see doweling page 57).

Repeat steps 1 through 17
to make the footboard.

Side Rails

STEP 18.

Cut to length two side rails, using 5-6 inch diameter logs. In the same way you put tenons on your cross pieces, use a 2 5/8 inch dowel plug cutter and put a 2 inch long tenon on both ends of each side rail.

STEP 19.

Verify the four mortise markings for the side rails and adjust as needed. (a queen bed will be 60" center to center) Drill the four mortise using a 2 5/8 inch saw tooth bit and drill 2 inches deep.

STEP 20.

While the head and foot board are still laying on the ground, use a 3/8 inch auger bit to drill a pilot hole for the lag bolts in the center of the four mortises. Drill all the way through the post.

STEP 21.

Turn the headboard/footboard over. Using a 1 1/2 inch drill bit, drill a countersink hole 5/8 inch deep for the washer and head of the lag bolt. You will make a plug to fit the hole later in step 26.

STEP 22.

Stand the headboard up. Insert the side rails into the mortise in the headboard, then into the footboard. Secure using 6 inch lag bolts with washers. We use a half inch drive electric impact wrench to drive tighten these bolts.

STEP 24.

Notching the side rails

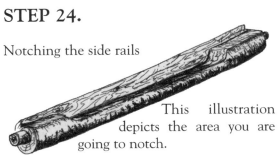

This illustration depicts the area you are going to notch.

Basically, you are cutting a 45 degree section out of the log. You are making the frame your mattress and box spring will set into.

To mark out the side rail notch, you will need a tape and chalk line.

2 x 4 Slats

With slats in place, use a board to find this line.

Scribe with a marker then cut and grind. (See end view illustration below.)

End view of notched rail

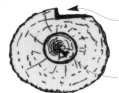

This area must be cut or ground down to match the height of the 2 x 4 slats

Tenon

STEP 25.

Make sure the bed is square. check the head board relationship to the foot board. Adjust where needed

Cut 3 to 4 2x4 slats 60 inches long. place slats across the span of the notched out bed rails. if they don't fit. check your width. Try turning the side rails out a bit, increasing the span. This might give you the extra 1/2 inch or so that you need.

Making Plugs.

STEP 26.

Using 2- 2 1/2 inch diameter log, place a half inch long tenon on both ends. (we use both ends for speed and ease in making multiple plugs.

STEP 27.

Using a 7/8 to 1 inch drill bit, drill a 1/2 inch deep hole in the center.

This hole will fit around the 3/4 inch head of the lag bolt.

STEP 28.

Cut the plug 1/8 inch past the beginning of the taper

STEP 29.

Clean, sand and be sure they fit snug against the post. If they don't shorten the length of the hollow tenon on the plug.

STEP 30.

Check over the bed for any glue spots or areas that need sanding. Congratulations, you have just built your first log bed - Sign it or Stamp with your name, and your ready to put on the finish. (See Finishes page 67).

alf log tables have a lot of character and are very popular. This type of table is a piece of log furniture that could be found in a cabin deep in the mountains or a working ranch in the valley. Actually, this table is perfect for any home looking for that genuine rustic look and can be built from pine, aspen or whatever wood you have access to. Remember that the wood needs to be soft enough for your cutting tools to cut. Most tables of this type are built from aspen because of its color and character.

Building a half log table is a challenge. This is definitely one of the more advanced projects in this book. For the purpose of this book, the dimensions of the table we are going to illustrate for you is approximately 24 inches wide, 48 inches long, and 30 inches actual table height. If you want to build a wider table, increase the width of the two ends. For a longer table, increase the length of the table sidepieces. Or you can calculate a combination of both.

Splitting logs

Building half log tables requires that someone split/cut logs down the center into two pieces. We recommend you check with your local mill or lumber yard and have them split/cut your logs for you.

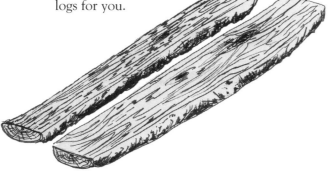

If you are somewhat experienced and have a helping hand you can get out the ban saw and cut your logs. We typically use a band saw to cut our logs in half.

If you are very experienced with a chain saw you can put on your thinking cap and get a bit creative. Splitting logs in half is not an easy task, but practice makes perfect. We have included some basic instructions for cutting logs in half with a chain saw. Again this is not for the inexperienced chain saw user.

Place the log you want to split on your horse and strap it down to hold it securely. This log should be quite a bit longer than the finished size needed.

Place a level on the end of the log. Eyeball the center and draw a line, do the same on the other end.

Next, chalk a line down the center of the log on both the top and bottom. (see illustration at the top of page 135)

CUT LIST

4 . Table legs @ 33 inches
(5-6 inches in diameter)

2 Table end cross pieces
@ 13 inches (4 inches in diameter)

1 Log, split in half for Table top center pieces
@ 48 inches (6 inches in diameter)

1 Log, split in half for Tabletop side pieces
@ 35 inches (6 inches in diameter)
(one half for each side of the Tabletop)

STEP 1.

Follow the cut list, cut and mark all your pieces.

STEP 2.

Peel and sand your logs.

STEP 3.

Put tenons on the following pieces .
For this project, we recommend a 2-inch diameter tenon, 2 inches long.

Cut a 2-inch tenon on each end of the 35-inch long table top side pieces.

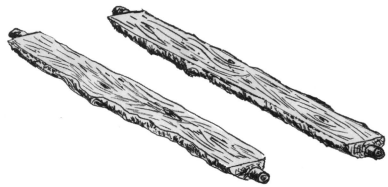

Now cut the log in half. You will cut part of the way down the log then you will need to move the strap and finish the cutting. When cutting the log in half, try to watch carefully and follow the lines on both sides of the log for a straight and level cut. This is going to take some practice. Chain saws seldom make a smooth cut, but don't be concerned you can come back later with your angle grinder and smooth out any rough spots.

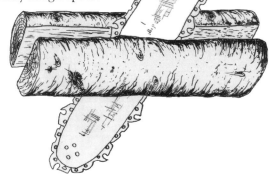

Put 2-inch tenons on each end of the two 13-inch pieces.

Step 4.

On each of the four table legs measure up from the bottom (the bigger end of the log) 26 inches and make a mark for the mortise placement.

Step 5.

Using a 2-inch forstner bit or saw tooth bit, drill a 2-inch deep mortise (hole) in each leg.

Step 6.

Assemble the end section by placing a 13-inch table end cross pieces, with tenons on each end, into the mortise on each leg.

Repeat to assemble the opposite end section.

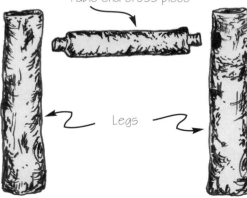

Table end cross piece

Legs

Step 8.

On the inside of each completed table end section measure up from the bottom of each leg 29 inches. Mark the placement of the mortise for the top side pieces. Using your 2-inch bit, drill all four holes 2 inches deep.

Remember, do not intersect the 29 inch mortise and the mortise of the Table end cross piece

Step 9.

Frame out the table by connecting the completed table end sections with the two 35 inch half log table top side pieces. You should have put tenons on each end of these pieces in step three.

Step 10.

Check to ensure everything is level and the table legs are straight up and down, glue and dowel all 8 tenons using 5/8 inch dowel.

With the table framed out, you are ready to put in the half log table top center pieces.

Step 11.

In the next few steps you will be cupping or notching out each table end cross piece This will enable the half log table top center pieces to recess into the table end cross pieces making the surface height of the half log table top center pieces match the surface height of the half log table top side pieces.

Step 12.

Lay both 48-inch half log table top center pieces across the table.

Measure the difference from the top of the half log table top center pieces down to the top of the half log table top side pieces. That is the depth you will need to notch out.

Step 13.

Set your scribe to the depth measurement and scribe your mark onto the table end cross piece. Repeat for both ends of each half log table top center log.

Step 14.

Cup or notch out the scribed area. We have shown some of the tools below which you can use to accomplish this task. If you don't have the tools shown, you can most likely improvise with what ever tools you do have on hand.

The illustrations below show the notches being cut out to cup the log.

Notice we make a cut, leave a narrow space, and then make another cut.

Each cut is made down to our scribe mark.

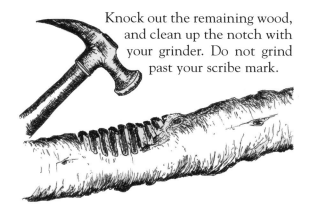

Knock out the remaining wood, and clean up the notch with your grinder. Do not grind past your scribe mark.

Step 15.

Now that you have saddle notched the space for your table top center pieces, set them in place and see how they fit.

Remember, working with logs means there will be irregularities and gaps between the logs. Use your grinder and make any adjustments necessary. If you have quarter inch to half-inch gaps, it's not the end of the world. Your table will have character and be more rustic. It is up to you as the builder to do what is pleasing to the eye. You get to decide when enough is enough and just let the rest go.

Step 16.

When your satisfied with the appearance of your table top, glue and dowel into place your table top center pieces using 5/8-inch dowel.

Step 17.

Grind and sand table top to your liking. Check over the rest of your table for any glue or rough spots and grind or sand them out.

Congratulations, you just built your first half log table. You're ready to put on a finish. (See Finishes page 57).

Resources

A. J. Images Inc. Communications Design
http://www.ajimagesinc.com

Amazon.com, Online Book Store
http://www.amazon.com

Campbell Hausfeld
http://www.chpower.com

Dick Blick Art Materials
http://www.dickblick.com

Fine Woodworking Magazine
http://www.taunton.com/fw/

Joe Vitale
Knowledge Site
http://www.mrfire.com/

Lookout Below Productions
http://www.lookoutbelow.net

Minwax Wood Finishing Sourcebook
http://www.minwax.com

Masterfx
http://www.masterfx.com

Titebond Glue
http://www.titebond.com
Franklin International
http://www.franklin.com
http://www.FranklinAdhesives.com

USDA Forest Service
http://www.fs.fed.us
Search for National Forests by map, by state,
by region, or by name
http://www.fs.fed.us/links/other.shtml

COLORADO'S
Beautiful
Forest
Resources

THE WOOD PRODUCTS INDUSTRY AND HEALTHY COMMUNITIES

reprinted with permission of Raul Bustamante
United Wood Products, Longmout, CO.

For generations, the woods products industry, ranching and farming, sustained many communities. Many towns were originally located close to the supply of the renewable timber resource. During the mining boom, forests provided mine props and lumber for building towns. Train tracks were laid on railroad ties from the forest. Firewood heated homes and was used for cooking. Poles were used for building fences to contain livestock.

Today, thousands of people across the country are directly employed in the primary manufacture of wood products. These includes loggers, truckers and mill workers who produce lumber, beams, railroad ties, paneling, house logs, wafer board, posts, poles and firewood. Additionally, thousands are employed by secondary manufacturing companies that make products such as furniture, cabinets and trusses. All these workers collect wages which go into the economy to support families; they own homes and automobiles, pay taxes, buy groceries and contribute to the social well-being of their community.

THE FOREST

The forests have evolved over thousands of years in which natural fire has played a significant role. Native Americans burned thousands of acres every year to improve their hunting grounds. By the late 1800s, fire suppression was organized and aggressive and a drastic reduction in forest fires can be traced to 1870. Many forces other than fire have contributed to the present forest condition, which is unlike the forest of our forefathers. These forces include: widespread livestock grazing, reduction of the native plant and wildlife populations by settlers and the introduction and spread of non-native species. More recently, residential development has sharply increased within the forest and the pressure is increasing. The results of these changes include: different tree size and species distribution, and older trees than occur naturally.

The number of trees that die from insects or disease is increasing. The amount of dead and dying trees, or fuel load, is also increasing. Records indicate that fires of today burn more intensely than those in the past. With the absence of regular fire, the average age of the forest is increasing and fewer trees are naturally regenerating. Some species such as ponderosa pine and Douglas-fir require bare mineral soil for a seed bed to reproduce. Fire actually encourages lodge pole pine reproduction. What does all this mean for the forest of our future? Harvest and prescribed fire are the tools we can use to shape the healthy forests of the future. More and more people are realizing that we must make sensible decisions and incorporate sound management to insure the continued viability of our forested ecosystem, to protect our investments and insure a continuing supply of wood products.

All of us want to shape a healthier environment to pass down to the next generation. We are continually improving forest management techniques by learning from the past. The forest industry is a tool for the management of our forests. Careful removal of trees will provide forest products while enabling reintroduction of low intensity fire. The whole forest can be managed for objectives such as: insect control, disease prevention, providing a sustained supply of forest products, maintaining healthy forest ecosystem, and ecological restoration.

THE SUSTAINABLE AND RENEWABLE FOREST

There is no substitute for the way that wood fits into our lives and makes us feel. It is renewable, biodegradable and recyclable. So many products like chemicals for medicine, lumber, furniture, plastics, paper products, film and rayon are made from wood. Producing wood for building materials is much more energy efficient that the production of other materials. Growing trees gives off oxygen while they take in carbon dioxide, and unlike metals and fossil fuels, wood from a managed forest is a readily renewable resource. Trees are a wonderful source of raw material because they naturally regenerate and provide a continuous supply. National forests are managed to provide a sustained flow of many multiple benefits. These are derived in an integrated manner from all forests lands meeting a portion of our nation's demand for wood, water, forage, wildlife, and outdoor recreation opportunities.

(Careful management and harvesting of our forests will provide wood products for our needs and beautiful forests for future generations.)

Notes:

_____

_____

_____

_____

_____

_____

_____

_____

_____

_____

_____

Notes:

_____   _____

_____   _____

_____   _____

_____   _____

_____   _____

_____   _____

_____   _____

_____   _____

_____   _____

_____   _____

_____   _____

_____   _____

_____   _____

_____   _____

_____   _____

_____   _____

National Forestry List

Alabama Forestry Commission
513 Madison Ave.
Montgomery, AL 36130
205-240-9304

Alaska Division of Forestry
400 Willoughbury Ave.
Juneau, AK 99801
907-561-2020

Arizona State Land Dept.
1616 West Adams
Phoenix, AZ 85007
602-255-4621

Arkansas Forestry Commission
P.O. Box 4523 - Asher Station
Little Rock, AR 72214
501-664-2531

California Dept. of Forestry & Fire Protection
Resource Building
P.O. Box 94246
Sacramento, CA 94244-2460

Colorado State Forrest Service
203 Forestry Bldg.
Colorado State University
Fort Collins, CO 80523
970-491-6303

Connecticut Bureau of Forestry
Dept. of Environmental Protection
165 Capital Ave.
912-744-3237

Delaware Dpt. of Agriculture
2320 South Dupont Highway
Dover, DE 19901
302-736-4811

Florida Division of Forestry
3125 Conner Blvd.
Tallahassee, FL 32399-1650
904-448-4274

Georgia Forestry Commission
P.O. Box 819
Macon, GA 31298-4599
912-744-3237

Guam Forestry & Natural Resources
P.O. Box 9250
Agana, GU 96010
671-734-3948

Hawaii Division of Forestry & Wildlife
1151 Punch bowl Street
Honolulu, HI 96813
808-548-8850

Idaho Dept. of Lands
State Capitol Bldg. R-121
Boise, ID 83720
208-334-3284

Illinois Dept. of Natural Resources
Northwest Office Plaza
600 North Grand Ave.
West Springfield, IL 62706

Indiana Dept. of Natural Resources
Division of Forestry
613 State Office Bldg.
Indianapolis, IN 46204
317-232-4105

Iowa Dept. of Natural Resources
Wallace State Office Bldg.
Des Moines, IA 50319
515-281-8656

Kansas Dept. of Forestry
2610 Claflin Rd.
Manhattan, KS 66502
913-537-7050

Kentucky Division of Forestry
627 Comanche Trail
Frankfort, KY 40601
502-564-4496

Louisiana Dept. of Agriculture
Office of Forestry
P. O. Box 1628
Baton Rouge, LA 70821
504-925-4500

Maine Dept. of Conservation
Bureau of Forestry
State House Station 822
Augusta, GA
207-289-2791

Maryland Forest, Park and Wildlife Service
Tawes State Office Building
580 Taylor Ave.
Annapolis, MD 21401
301-974-3776

Massachusetts Div. of Forests and Parks
Dept. of Environmental Mgmt.
100 Cambridge St.
Boston, MA 02202
617-727-3180

Forest Management Division
Michigan Dept. of Natural Resources
Steven T. Mason Bldg.
P.O. Box 30028
Lansing, MI 48909
517-373-1275

Minnesota Division of Forestry
500 Lafayette Rd.
St. Paul, MN 55155-4044
612-296-4484

Mississippi Forestry Commission
301 Building Suite 300
Jackson, MS 39201
601-359-1356

Missouri Dept. of Conservation
2901 West Truman Blvd.
P. O. Box 180
Jefferson City, MO 54102
314-751-4115

Montana Dept. of Forestry
Dept. of State Lands
2705 Spurgin Rd.
Missoula, MT 59801
406-542-4300

Nebraska Dept. of Forestry
Fisheries & Wildlife
Room 101 Plant Industries Bldg.
Lincoln, NE 68583
402-472-2944

Nevada Division of Forestry
201 South Fall St.
Canon City, NV 89701
701-885-4350

New Hampshire
Division of Forests and Land
Box 856, Prescott Park
Concord, NH 03301-0856
603-271-2214

New Jersey State Forestry
CN 404, 501 E. State St.
Station Plaza #5
Trenton, NJ 08625
609-984-3850

New Mexico Forestry Division
P.O. Box 2167
Santa Fe, NM 87504-2167
505-827-5830

New York Division of Lands and Parks
Dept. of Environmental Conservation
50 Wolf Road
Albany, NY 12233-4250

North Carolina Div. of Forest Resources
P.O. Box 27687
Raleigh, NC 27611-7687
919-733-2162

North Dakota Forest Service
First and Brander
Bottineau, ND 58318
701-228-2277 ext. 290

Ohio Division of Forestry
Fountain Square
Columbus, OH 43224
614-265-6690

Oklahoma Dept. of Agriculture
Forestry Division
2800 N. Lincoln Blvd.
405-521-3864

Oregon Dept. of Forestry
2600 State St.
Salem, OR 97310
503-378-2511

Pennsylvania Bureau of Forestry
P.O. Box 1467
Harrisburg, PA 17120
717-787-2703

Puerto Rico Dept. of Natural Resources
809-724-3647

Rhode Island
Div. of Forest Environment
1037 Hartford Pike
North Scituate, RI 02857
402-847-3367

South Carolina
Forestry Commission
P.O. Box 21707
Columbia, SC 29221
803-737-8800

Tennessee Dept. of Conservation
Division of Forestry
701 Broadway
Nashville, TN 37219-5237
615-742-6616

Texas Forest Service
College Station, TX 77843-2136
409-845-2641

Utah Division of State Lands & Forestry
3 Triad Center #400
Salt Lake City, UT 84180-1204
801-537-3100

Vermont Dept. of Forestry
103 S. Main St., 10 South
Waterbury, VT 05676
802-244-8711

Virgin Islands Dept. of Forestry
King Field Post Office
St. Croix, VI 00851
809-778-0997

Virginia Division of Forestry
P.O. Box 3758
Charlottesville, VA
804-977-6555

Washington Dept. of Natural Resources
201 John A. Cherberg Bldg.
Mail Stop QW-21
Olympia, WA 98504

West Virginia Forestry Division
State Capitol Charleston, WV 53707
304-348-2788

Wisconsin Chief Forester
P.O. Box 7921
Madison, WI
608-266-0842

Wyoming State Forestry
1100 West 22nd St.
Cheyenne, WY 82002
307-777-7586

Resources & Contacts:

_____   _____
_____   _____
_____   _____
_____   _____
_____   _____
_____   _____
_____   _____
_____   _____
_____   _____
_____   _____
_____   _____
_____   _____
_____   _____
_____   _____

ENCYCLOPEDIA OF WOOD: A TREE-BY- TREE GUIDE TO THE WORLDS MOST VALUABLE RESOURCE *by William Lincoln, Aidan Walker, John Makepeace, Bill Lincoln, Lucinda Leech, Luke Hughes.* Checkmark Books 1989 ISBN#0-81602-159-7

FINE WOODWORKING ON WOOD AND HOW TO DRY IT. Taunton Press 1986s ISBN #0-918804-54-X

IDENTIFYING WOOD ACCURATE RESULTS WITH SIMPLE TOOLS *by R. Bruce Hoadley* Taunton Books 1991 ISBN #0-942391-04-7

THE WOODCUTTERS GUIDE: CHAINSAWS, WOODLOTS, AND PORTABLE SAWMILLS by *Dave Johnson*, Chelsea Green Publishing Company 1998 ISBN #1-89013-215-2

THERE'S A CUSTOMER BORN EVERY MINUTE: P.T. BARNUM'S SECRETS TO BUSINESS SUCCESS, *by Joseph G. Vitale*, AMACOM 1998 ISBN# 0-81447-953-7

UNDERSTANDING WOOD A CRAFTSMAN'S GUIDE TO WOOD TECHNOLOGY by *R. Bruce Hoadley*, 20th-anniversary edition Taunton Press 2000 ISBN #1-56158-358-8

Glossary

Adz, hand tool used to make saddle notch *(see tools of yesterday)*

Arch, curved form

Auger, boring tool, drill bit *(see tools of yesterday)*

Backing Pad, accessory for angle grinder *(see tools of today)*

Bark, outer layer of tree covering

Barn Wood, used weathered wood

Beetle Kill, disease that kills pine trees (metallic back beetle, etc.)

Bind, term used when the drill bit sticks or grabs, stopping the drill.

Cats Paw, While alive, the bark is torn away. The tree continues to grow and recover, but leaves a scar.

Case Goods, Term used for a piece of furniture with doors or drawers

Character, combination of qualities, style

Checking, Natural process of cracking while the wood releases it's moisture.

Chuck, the part of the drill that holds and tightens the drill bit

Cleat, used to support or build up, used to attach shelves etc.

Consignment, to turn merchandise over to another for sale; craftsman is paid when merchandise is sold.

Creak, this sound indicates weak or loose jointed furniture

Cross Piece, horizontally positioned logs, closely related to rungs

Cup, equal warping, cup or bowl shaped

Cut List, number, length and diameter of logs and boards needed to complete a project

Cutting Tools, Instruments used to drill, cut and shape wood

Dehumidification, To remove the moisture, water weight from timber or lumber

Diameter, width or the length across

Disk, round, gritty sand paper/grinder disks, replaceable

Dowel, length of wood rod, various sizes *(see doweling)*

Doweling, tying or locking the tenon together, used to connect boards in making tops

Draw Knife, cutting/shaping tool used to remove bark, shape wood (tenon), finishing

Dry Kiln, used to dry lumber or timbers to the proper moisture content, dehumidification process for wood

Dry Wood, lumber/timbers with a moisture content of 12% or less

Drill Press, table top drill, engaged with a lever, adjustable speeds

Finish, oil base, water base applications to treat, protect and hi-light wood color and grain

Flat Shoulder Tenon, *(see tenon and mortise section)*

Flush, even with, level

Gnarly (nar-lee), Term used to describe a combination of rustic qualities (gnarls/burls)

Grinding, to form , shape, remove, scuff and clean wood

Half Inch Drive, the size of drill shank the chuck will accept typically 3/8 or half inch

Hard Wood, wood that comes from broad leaf trees, dense

Hexed Shank, a multi-sided drill bit shank, reduces slippage in the chuck

High Lines, term used to describe the lines or high rows left by the draw knife

Humidity, percentage of moisture in the surrounding air

Imaginary Straight Line, *(see tenon & mortise section for illustration)*

Joint, where two pieces meet and are connected

Lag Bolts, large screws, bolt style without the nut, used with a washer

Leveling, term used to describe the evening of legs to level, to be even with

Locking Nut, attaches the backing pad to the angle grinder

Log Furniture, furniture fashioned from timbers and rough sawn materials

Lumber Mill, site used to cut timbers into lumber

Moisture Content, percentage of moisture/water inside wood

Mortise (more-dus), hole, equal to length and diameter of dowel or tenon

Peeling, remove bark

Pivot, to turn, spin, twist loose

Pulls, handles

Radius Tenon, *(see tenon & mortise section)*

Round Shank, round drill bit from end to end

RPM, number of rotation, rounds, revolutions per minute

Rough Sawn Boards, rough cut lumber, inconsistent thickness and length, saw blade marks are visible

Rung, step of a ladder, term to describe cross piece, typically horizontal, a bridge

Rustic, term used to describe the attractive characteristics, anomalies, appreciated natural features inherent in furniture fashioned and born out of natures timbers and rough cut, rough sawn lumber.

Saddle Notch, cup out, notch wood in the shape of a saddle, quarter moon shape

Sanding, to smooth the surface of wood, remove marks, preparation for finishing

Saw Horse, *(see work stations)*

Saw Mill, actual bladed sawing station to cut trees into lumber

Saw Tooth, individual cutting blade, or sharp burr making up a saw blade

Shank, part of the drill bit inserted into the chuck of the drill *(see mortise & tenon for illustration)*

Single Edge Boards, Rough sawn lumber with one edge cut straight, one edge with bark

Spindle, Similar to rungs, spindles are set vertical

Split, a crack or check in wood

Slabs, different than un-edged or single edge boards, slabs are the four corners of the tree with bark on

Soft Wood, wood from cone bearing trees, pine, aspen

Structural Integrity, overall strength, safe for load bearing purposes

Taper, to decrease in size gradually, as the pencil comes to a point with a gradual taper

Tapered Tenon, *(see tenon and mortise section)*

Tenon, tapered or round dowel like length of wood used to join furniture, *(see tenon & mortise section)*

Timber, harvested trees ready to be cut into lumber

Top Coat, the outer protective layer or coat of finish (some sort of urethane)

Tops, *(see making tops)*

Un-edged Boards, no straight edge has been cut, bark on both sides of the board, middle cut or rip of tree

Vice, *(see work stations)*

Warp, bend or gradual twist in lumber, semi cupped

Wet Wood, lumber or timbers that contain 13% or more moisture/water

Wobble, loose, not steady, not stable, not level, teeters

Work Station, apparatus designed to assist the worker in completing a certain application of tools
(see Section 3 getting started, work stations)

Index